Funny, Sexy, Nanobots (and other improvements)

The Simple Displeasures Collection
- Volume One -

By Peter Wick

© 2006, 2007, 2008, 2009, 2010, 2011, 2012, 2013, 2014, 2015, 2016, 2017 by Peter Wick

"The Truth About Snow White," "The Writings of Dr. Pleuss," and "The Salvador Deli" appear for the first time in this collection.

Cover design and interior formatting by Ross Denyer

Cover drawing by Peter Wick

Also by Peter Wick

FILMS

Long Strange Trip (Director, Writer, Actor – 1999)

- "Wick scores high with this wry road trip movie." – Seattle Weekly review, 1999

- "Most Promising Director" Award, NYIIFVF, 1999

- On several lists of Longest Movie Titles of all Time – (Full title is "Long Strange Trip – Or The Writer, The Naked Girl, and The Guy With a Hole In His Head.")

(Available at www.indieflix.com)

Movie Pizza Love (Director, Writer, Actor – 2008)

- Indiefest Award-Of-Merit Winner
- On several "favorite Films" lists around the world

(available on Amazon video and DVD)

Rock Paper Scissors (Director, Writer, Actor – 2011)

- Accolade Competition winner
- Best Director – NYIFF – 2011

(available on Amazon video and DVD)

www.peter-wick.com

Twitter: @juventinopw

Simple Displeasures: www.peterwick.blogspot.com

Youtube: Azzurri Productions

BOOKS

Key West – Special Edition (Key West Novel – 2013 – plus prequel short story "The King of the Keys" - 2015)

"An engaging fun read," -Mark Howell, Key West Citizen

"Cannot put it down." -Amazon customer review

"Borders on 'riveting'." -Amazon customer review

Key West – The Companion Episodes (Wick's kindle-only 2013 and 2014 "Companion Episodes" together under one cover for the first time - 2015)

-5 out of 5 stars

- "I love the setting and the characters." -Janelle Fila, Readers Favorite

It Is What It Is – A novella (2015)

"Readers will follow the flow and enjoy this tale." -Dick Weissman, Portland Book Review

Funny, Sexy Nanobots
Contents

Part One: Before Simple Displeasures

1. The Truth About Snow White – By Sneezy — 10
2. Now in 4-D! — 13
3. Travels with Bailey and Bella — 15
4. Cecil Grant — 17
5. Tripstix, Mookie, and Footloose — 19
6. Searching for the RIGHT Scandal — 21
7. Not All Oscar Fantasies are Created Equal — 23
8. The Writings of Dr. Pleuss — 25
9. Why is Love Always A Near Miss? (a story) — 29

Part Two: Simple Displeasures

10. Cheney Emails Declassified — 35
11. Sexy Girls on Motorcycles — 37
12. Gay Divorce — 39
13. The Guy Who Saves String — 41
14. Violence — 43
15. Democrats, Republicans, and Aliens from Outer Space — 45
16. Curiosity — 46
17. Free Pussy Riot — 48
18. Bob Dylan's Dentist — 50
19. To Brit or Not to Brit — 51
20. I am Not a Bank Robber — 53
21. Places on Earth — 55
22. The Peacefulness of the Ungoverned — 57
23. The Middle of Somewhere — 59
24. Brothers — 61
25. Chris Farley — 63
26. Cobain/Van Gogh — 66

27. Soccer, Noses, and Doctor's Advice	68
28. Rising Waters	70
29. Customer Service	72
30. The Cosby Concept	76
31. The Once and Future Sonics	79
32. Abducted	81
33. Social Media Has Saved the World	83
34. Funny, Sexy, Nanobots	85
35. Awards Season	87
36. VOTE for the Absurd Ideas Party!	89
37. Fools	91
38. May 5th; A National Day of…Prayer/Reason/Drinking	93
39. Report From Planet Earth	95
40. Drunk Brits	97
41. The Trump University Course Catalog	99
42. An Open Letter To Hackers	101
43. Happy National Cheese Curd Day	103
44. The Ghosts of Elections Past and Future	105

Part Three: The Salvador Deli (a story)   **109**

Part One:
before
Simple Displeasures

(So...does this mean things were less simple, or that they were more pleasurable?)

1

The Truth About Snow White

(By Sneezy)

I want to clear the air about one thing; I don't sneeze all that much.

I admit I have a few allergies, pollen is not my friend, dust is annoying, but I live a normal life.

I do now, anyway, now that I've moved on, now that Doc is put away.

Doc named us. You can tell, too. Look at the name he gave himself compared to the rest of us. Doc, as opposed to Bashful, or Dopey. I mean, come on! Dopey? You'd never know the ol' D-man was a physicist. He's a scientist, for crying out loud. Graduated from The University of Dwarford. Okay, he's a little absent-minded. What scientist isn't? So, one day he forgets his coat and Doc tags him with the name Dopey. Life just isn't fair.

For the record, my real name is Laurence. Dopey's is Harold. Doc's was Lucinda – now you know why he wanted to change our names.

As or Snow White, I know I'm going to hear from some haters for saying this, but she was totally f---ing crazy.

The first example came the very first moment we saw her. She was asleep in our bedroom. We had just come home from a hard day digging in the pit (please don't get me started about that damn pit Doc was obsessed with), and it seemed a little strange that some rich chick was sleeping in our house.

So we woke her up. She threw a fit. She acted like we had invaded her privacy. She stomped around yelling and then she went downstairs in a huff.

Then...she started cleaning.

She cleaned compulsively. She straightened everything up. I could no longer find my favorite books. Dopey couldn't find a Physics paper he'd been writing. (He had been working to expound on Einstein's Theory of Relativity; for years he had been trying to prove that not only are two objects relative to each other in space and time, but that they will also make a loud popping sound if you whack them together suddenly.)

Doc put the pressure on, though, and Dopey and I settled for muttering under our breath.

If you only know the popularized fairy tale version of what happened, you would probably expect Grumpy to be the most upset of all.

Don't believe it.

Sure, Doc named him Grumpy because he got a little upset now and then. Who doesn't? Really, he was a softy. The Grump, as we called him, was a character, a round pudgy guy who tended to be goofy. When he did get upset he was so unsure of himself, he hardly had the will to yell at anyone.

Snow White stayed in our house that night. Doc told her she could. Personally, I questioned Doc's motives, but kept it to myself.

That night she took over the bedroom and wouldn't let us in, not even to get our toothbrushes. Doc took the couch, and the rest of us had to curl up on the floor in sleeping bags. It was a miserable night. I tossed and turned, and when I finally did doze off I had a vivid dream that I was a dragon, and that I was delighted to breathe fire on Doc and Snow White. In the dream, I was still myself, while also being a dragon, though, and unsure how to handle my own fire-breath, I scorched the inside of my nose and mouth, and flew away screaming and in horrible pain.

Then Doc shook us all awake for another day digging in the pit.

I still don't know what he was trying to accomplish in that pit. There was nothing there. We were just digging, day after day, and the dust we stirred up was messing with my allergies.

Off we went every morning, mumbling that god-forsaken song, that annoying "Hi-ho" thing. If I ever hear that song again, I swear I'm going to hurt someone.

Now, I have to be careful what I say about Snow White and that sleeping potion. I don't want to sound cruel, but I have to be honest.

When we came home from the pit that night and found her unconscious, most of us weren't exactly in tears.

Doc was the only who really cared, and he went overboard with it. He was obsessed. He built her that ridiculous golden bed to lie on. He stayed with her day and night. It wasn't healthy. The man was losing it.

Then, as everyone knows, Prince In-bred (I mean 'Charming') came by and kissed her and she woke up.

You know what happened next; she married him, went off to live the life of a Princess in a castle, bore him an heir, gradually they grew distant, she began having an affair with the gardener, and finally quit the royal family in a sensational scandal (if you want to go on believing they lived 'happily ever after,' fine, believe it).

As for the seven of us, it was never the same after the Snow White affair. Doc never got over her. He brooded and sulked for months, sinking into an alcoholic stupor. He even lost interest in the pit. He would just sit around the house all day, drunkenly stumbling from one room to another, mumbling, "Hi...ho...hi..hic..ho..." and collapsing onto the floor in a passed out heap. Finally one day he went mad and tried to tear the place apart, so we called the authorities and had him put away.

Then the rest of us slowly went our separate ways and lost touch with each other.

I ran into Bashful recently. He seemed happy. He was working as a male stripper in Las Vegas ('Bashful' was never the best name for him, either). He mentioned something about Grumpy living under a bridge somewhere in the Swiss Alps.

I stay in touch with Dopey. We're still close. He finished his research and published his findings in a highly acclaimed book titled, "The New Relativity Diet; The Space Travel Weight Loss System" His ideas are insightful and ground-breaking, and I am convinced that if the book had been written by a non-dwarf, it's author would have won the Nobel Prize, either the Physics Prize, or certainly their Weight-loss prize. But, Dopey is a dwarf, of course, and dwarves just aren't taken seriously in the scientific community.

2
Now in 4-D!

(From the "Rock Paper Scissors" blogs, 2010-2011)

It is March, 2011.

I wanted to make a point of reminding everyone what the date is, because it won't be long until all movies will be made in 3-D.

In fact, pretty soon, the entire world will be in 3-D!

I have been doing some research into this 3-D phenomenon, and it turns out the "D" in 3-D stands for "Dimensions." The 3 dimensions people are talking about are "height," "width," and "depth." These three dimensions never existed until genius animators at Disney and Pixar invented them.

I can't wait until REAL LIFE is in 3-D!

Hm? What? What was that?....Could you say that one more time, please?

I have just been told that REAL LIFE has been in 3 dimensions since the beginning of time....and speaking of time, I have also been told that according to some bloke named Einstein, the FOURTH dimension is time!

Do you know what this discovery means?! It means that we have been living - not in 3-D - in 4-D since the beginning of time!

This is stunning news. This is a game changer!

This means that when I go see the live theater production of Steinbeck's "Of Mice and Men," later this month, it will be in 4-D!

Seriously, think about it, live theater happens in real time, in front of you, with live Actors over the course of a period of TIME.

LIVE THEATER IS IN 4-D!

If an Actor decides to run off the stage, directly at you, it will look and feel like he actually IS running directly at you. Why? Because IT IS ACTUALLY HAPPENING!

Live theater has been in 4-D since the Greeks, thousands of years ago.

And you don't have to wear funny glasses.

I can't handle this stunning news.

Just imagine how excited today's younger generation will be when they discover that REAL LIFE is in 4-D.

The kids will be beside themselves, clamoring to experience real life. They won't be able to get enough of it. Forget video games. Forget 3-D movies. Real life is where it will be AT in the future.

The poor grownups, though. What will they think of it?

"I remember back in the day, when all you had to do all day was play a 2-D video game. It was all we had. And we liked it!"

"Yep, you got that right, Mortimer. 2-D was enough for us back then. Who needs all this real life in 4-D stuff?"

"These kids today!"

"Yeah, these kids, with their reality, and all the dimensions. It's NONSENSE, I tell you."

Live Theater will overtake movies in a landslide. Movies...who needs 'em? Live Theater is in 4-D, just like real life!

Hold on, people, the future is going to blow you away!

3

Travels with Bailey and Bella

(January, 2008)

When I drove from Seattle to L.A. last April, I left some unfinished business along the way. I hurried through central California, skipping Salinas, apologizing to John Steinbeck on my way past.

This past Fall I found myself involved in a conversation with some friends, asking the question, "Who is your most hated American novelist?" When someone said John Steinbeck, I had to jump in. "Have you read 'Travels with Charlie?'" I asked. "Have you read 'Cannery Row'? 'Sweet Thursday'?"

Sure, I admit "The Grapes of Wrath" is a little ponderous, but read those other three books, and I defy you to hate him.

So I stopped in Salinas this time, on my way up the coast in December. In "Travels With Charlie" Steinbeck mourns the encroaching touristy-ness of Salinas, and that was in 1960. He was fondly remembering a lost Salinas of 40 or 50 years earlier. So as I walked through 'old-town' Salinas, I wondered what he would think of the place today. I visited The Steinbeck Center, an odd sort of museum that sells t-shirts with quotes from his books on them. I doubted seriously whether Steinbeck would approve of that place.

3 weeks later I left Seattle and drove south again. The news warned me, before I left, that storms were moving in along the Oregon coast. I drove to meet those storms. They found me. They found me good.

Storms aren't enough, though. I had to add a bad right rear tire into the mix.

I knew my right rear tire would not last. A sensible person would have replaced it before the trip. I'm never quite satisfied, though, unless I know exactly how bad off something is. And you never really know how bad a tire is until...well...until a flap of its surface shreds off between Eugene and Florence and begins flapping loudly against the tire well as you drive.

This sound scared the cats to death (yes, I drove with my cats to Seattle for the holidays, and had them in the backseat of the car the whole way back). They had been dealing with the drive with a quietly annoyed acceptance. No longer.

I stopped the car, walked around the back, inspected the damage, saw that the tire was still holding air, and did what any sensible person would do in that situation; I ignored the problem, got back in the car, and started driving again.

30 minutes later, approaching the coast town of Florence, Oregon, the little tire flap that was making the awful noise (fwap, fwap, fwap, fwap) actually tore off on the road.

Suddenly the ride was quiet again.

"Cool," I thought. "I'll just keep driving."

That's when the first gust of near gale-force wind nearly lifted the car off the road and threatened to throw us into the woods nearby.

When the rain came, it wasn't really rain so much as a MONSOON.

Then hail started bouncing off the car like baseballs.

When lightning flashed nearby, the cats began preparing for what they assumed would be their final moments on Earth. Bella forgave Bailey for 3 years of unprovoked attacks, and they huddled together on the floor behind me seat, and prepared to die.

I drove for 3 hours in that storm, afraid to stop, certain that wherever I chose to turn the car off and spend the night, that was where I would have to buy a new tire in the morning.

The town was Crescent City, on the northern tip of the California coast.

Half the town had lost power. I slept in the car in the corner of a grocery store parking lot, two cats on top of me, the car rocking back and forth in the wind all night long.

I was the only customer at "Del Norte Tire" at 8 the next morning. I had walked several blocks to find the place. When I told Matt, and his boss Dan, my situation, and that overnight the tire had gone completely flat, Matt put some air in his portable air can and told me to climb into his pick-up truck. He drove me back to the grocery store parking lot, the local country station playing on the radio in the pick-up.

Matt put enough air in the tire for me to drive it back to the shop.

After putting the new tire on, Matt checked the air pressure in all my tires, tapped the right front, and said, "I'd keep my eye on that sum-m-bitch. I'd just keep my eye on it."

At 9 I drove away from "Del Norte Tire" with a brand new tire, a couple new friends – Matt, and his boss Dan, who seemed more interested in chatting than telling me what I owed him – and with a brand new appreciation for the town of Crescent City.

I want to go back sometime.

Of course I'll go back sometime.

And you know what? So will Bella and Bailey.

It will probably be summer, though, and the trip will no doubt be a lot less exciting.

4

Cecil Grant

(From the "Rock Paper Scissors" blogs – 2010-2011)

Cecil Grant died in 1951.

He suffered a heart attack. He was only 37 years old.

His entire body of work that survives is something like a dozen songs. He has now gone onto my list of all-time favorite musicians.

There is a short little scene in "Rock Paper Scissors," where I am sitting on the fishing boat that my character lives on, listening to the radio and doing a crossword puzzle. It is the end of the first day of the story. Marty has run into Lana for the first time since they were High School sweethearts many years ago.

When we shot the scene, we made a point of putting that portable radio in the shot. The technical processes of filmmaking dictated that we add whatever music Marty is listening to many months later, during post production.

So, when the film's editor, Everett Simila, and I came to that scene, during the editing process, I sort of procrastinated for several weeks. I wanted to go search for something. I wasn't sure what. I had in the back of my mind that Marty might be listening to jazz of some sort. Of course the legal world of music rights, combined with the production's lack of money at that point, narrowed our options quite a bit.

So one day I typed "Public domain jazz" into a search engine and found a little forgotten song from the 1940's that made me sit up and take notice.

It is called, "I Wonder," by Cecil Grant.

When I played it for Everett, and we synched it up with the scene, Everett and I looked at each other, a little bit speechless, smiling. We had found our song.

And as much as I tried to find the copyright owners, and the publishing rights owners, no one in the music world seems to claim the song.

I actually contacted Universal music publishing, who I had been told were the administrators of the song, and I got a perplexed sounding email back saying they did not know what song I was talking about and that it did not exist in their database.

It turns out that the record company has released the song directly to the public domain. I couldn't pay anyone for the rights, even if I wanted to (let's see if someone comes forward after reading this blog).

Cecil Grant wrote and sang blues and jazz with a boogie woogie piano style throughout the 1940's. Some of his songs were hits.

"I Wonder," was more of a ballad, a beautiful little piece, and was his biggest hit, in 1944.

He is almost completely forgotten now, unless I can do something about that right now.

Later in the day, after Everett and I placed the song over the scene, I played it for a female friend who was looking for songs that she could sing. She listened to it once. As soon as it ended, she pushed me out of the way, and said, "Sorry, I have to listen to this song, like five times in a row." then she sent a message to a piano player friend telling him to learn it fast, because it was her favorite new song.

So this is my way of giving back a little something to the memory of Cecil Grant, a forgotten artist, who died too young.

Long live Cecil!

5

Tripstix, Mookie, and Footloose

(from the "Rock Paper Scissors" blogs – 2010-2011)

Rock Paper Scissors is set in a High School, but it isn't a "High School Movie" the way Mean Girls is, or 10 Things I Hate About You.

It isn't in that genre of High School films where the students are the main characters.

High School is just a backdrop for a story involving Teachers.

Having said that, I get a lot of enjoyment from watching the High School Actors in the film. Shaq, Ayden, Olivia, Alison, Tellier, Molly, Samantha, are all great, and fun to watch on screen. They all brought some ideas of their own, and they all make the film better.

There is one scene, and two High School characters, who are not in the film, though, and I wish they were.

I didn't know either of them existed until last week. I was sitting, eavesdropping on their conversation at a Starbucks. The conversation went something like this:

Him: Oh, Dude, Tripstix is pissed at Footloose.

Her: Tripstix is such an ass.

Him: No, Dude, Footloose was freakin' last night.

Her: You guys were hangin' last night?

Him: Yeah, Tripstix was there, Footloose, Chipotle, Goober, and Mookie.

Her: Mookie was there?

Him: Yeah, Dude, Dude! Footloose is after Queen Bee and Tripstix is pissed.

Her: Queen Bee is a bitch.

Him: And Chipotle was tryin' to get with Goober.

Her: Oh my god, that's so stupid. What did Mookie do?

Him: Nothin.' Mookie doesn't like Chipotle anymore

Her: Nah! Mookie's all into Chipotle.

You get the basic idea; Tripstix and Footloose (who later turned out to be half-brothers) are mad at each other. Goober, Mookie, and Chipotle are stuck in a dysfunctional triangle, and Queen Bee is obviously the cause of a lot of jealousy.

I don't know the names of the two people who were having this conversation, although the girl was apparently "Dude."

I am giving the guy a nick name on my own. I have to put him into perspective, he can't remain nameless. He is now officially "Hi-Liter," because he had a streak in his hair similar to the color of a hi-liter pen I was using.

Good names, all of them; Tripstix, Footloose, Goober, Mookie, Chipotle, Dude, and Hi-Liter.

And from now on I would like you all to refer to me as "Glow Stick."

Watch what you say around me, though. I'm pissed at "Horse Shoe." Really really pissed. I can't stand that guy.

6
Searching for the RIGHT Scandal

(From the "Rock Paper Scissors" blogs, 2011)

When the good people at the New York International Film Festival gave me their "Best Director" Award last month, I was very happy at first.

Winning awards, though, is both a blessing and a curse. In today's world of "niche" marketing, where you target your audience by age, gender, education level, sexual preference, income level, religious belief, diet, and number of pimples on their body, I have had to humbly accept the fact that winning awards limits me to that tiny little "niche" audience who want to see "good" films.

This is devastating news to me.

I am being pigeon-holed as a "good" filmmaker. It's like a straightjacket that I can't break out of.

Or is it?

A friend on a social network recently messaged me with a comment that I am the "New Nick Nolte."

My response: "Do you mean that I will someday have a crazy-hair drunken mug shot splashed all over the tabloids? Yes! Can't wait!"

Then my friend said, "It's gonna happen sooner than you think."

I sure as hell hope so.

As today's society sprints toward proving Andy Warhol right, that in the future everyone will be famous for 15 minutes, it is important to think ahead, and decide what SORT of fame you want for your 15 minutes. I understand why those reading this would assume, "Well, Peter wants to be famous for making good films."

Absolutely not! What kind of fame would that be?

I am pursuing this dream with one simple truth in mind;

IT IS NEVER TOO EARLY TO BEGIN PLANNING YOUR SCANDAL!

Hollywood scandals are an art form all their own. Hugh Grant, in the 1990's, became famous for picking up a cheap Hollywood Boulevard hooker, and getting down to business in the car. This could not have been a less inspired, more boring choice on Mr. Grant's part.

Mel Gibson gave into the ho-hum trap of getting drunk and spewing racial nonsense to a bunch of Cops. Puh-lease! Mel, you aren't even TRYING!

Britney Spears had a more interesting scandal a few years back; she grabbed electric clippers from a hair stylist, and abruptly shaved half her hair off. This is more along the lines that inspires me. Maybe I have been around too many punk rock girls in my day, but I thought Britney looked ten times better half-bald than she usually does.

Nick Nolte did okay. He wasn't Christian Bale screaming at crew members or anything, but that mug shot is truly memorable. It is a start.

Give me time. I can't be expected to pull off a brilliant scandal overnight.

It will happen, though. I promise.

7
Not all Oscar Fantasies are created Equal

Someone asked me recently if I fantasize about winning Oscars.

I deflected the question.

I am not about to answer a question like that honestly.

I definitely DO fantasize about the Oscars, but as you will see, my fantasies are very different from most peoples.

When the question came up, I acted nonchalant and curmudgeonly, and complained about the Oscars being more about what people wear than about the films themselves. I went on to grumble about how I could never put on a tie, and as a consequence would probably never be let into the Oscars.

This is a serious problem, actually.

Whenever I see a man in a suit and tie, the only words in my head, loud and clear, drowning out everything else in there, is "Monkey suit!"

"Monkey suit!' over and over again and again. I begin imagining the man I'm looking at as a monkey, swinging from branch to branch, screeching in that uniquely ear-piercing monkey-like way.

You can see how serious a problem this is, in the context of watching the Oscars. The broadcast becomes a battle in my mind; Actor after Actor swinging and screeching until the entire Kodak Theater turns into an episode of "Animal Planet."

No man should ever wear a tie.

Here is my rule regarding ties: You should only tie something around your neck if you are planning to hang yourself.

If this is your plan, then I can understand and make an exception.

Someday, many years in the future, the Oscars will become a jeans and t-shirt affair. Maybe then I can go.

I am not completely against dress codes. I think pants are important. I think it would be reasonable for the Oscars to state clearly that any man not wearing pants will not be allowed into the ceremony.

I could support that rule.

You will also notice that I am not taking on women's fashion. I am too smart for that. If they want to go out there in many-thousand dollar gowns, god bless 'em.

As for the rest of my fantasy; I hesitate. This is dangerous territory.

Being honest about my fantasy in this regard could lose me some friends, maybe even some career opportunities. This is especially true if I begin explaining what I fantasize about doing on the night of the Oscars when I am nominated.

I fantasize about NOT GOING.

That's right.

Attending the Oscars, with those horrible E! Channel people on the red carpet, with all the botoxed faces and equally botoxed personalities...that would just be too horrible for words.

I want to be nominated, but since I know up front that they will not let me in, I think I'll pop down to some local bar, have a beer, watch an NBA basketball game, and find out later that night that I lost to George Clooney.

That's part of the fantasy; losing to George Clooney.

Please do not take any of this as being anti-Oscars. Seriously, I am big supporter of the whole idea behind the Oscars. Any time the film industry can celebrate something that goes beyond box office dollars - this can only be a good thing.

I just think, personally, having a beer and watching a basketball game would be a lot more fun than attending.

Besides, whenever that night comes, it will be George Clooney's night anyway.

8
The Writings of Dr. Pleuss

Perhaps it was the recent discovery of his deathbed confession that sent a buzz through the literary world. Maybe it was the unexpected circumstances surrounding the confession (Dr. Pleuss, gasping for breath, whispering to his 40-year-old son, who spent more time tugging at the ears of his rabbit suit than listening to his dying father). Maybe it was a combination of these two things. Whichever it was, the moment, mere seconds before Pleuss breathed his final breath, has changed the way we will look at children's literature forever.

When I heard the story in all its shocking details I felt I had gained a fleeting glimpse inside the mind of a literary genius; even the physician and nurses had dressed in rabbit suits, in an elaborate attempt to please the ailing author. Pleuss had clung stubbornly to his belief that rabbits can talk and, more importantly, perform difficult medical surgery.

Nothing stunned me quite so thoroughly, though, as the report of his dying confession, gasped quietly to his son. He admitted that, indeed, deeper meanings were hidden in his children's stories, and that the famous Green Mice themselves symbolized humanity's search for eternal truth. Or was it "Thermal Boots"? (Pleuss's son was struggling with the ears of his rabbit suit at the key moment, and didn't quite catch what the old man said.)

I picked out a volume or two of my Pleuss first editions, flipped through the pages, ran my fingers across the felt pasted onto the pictures of bears and monkeys. A new world of understanding was opening up to me. Was a dog merely a cute animal, as we had previously thought, or was Pleuss using it as a sly comment on European class structure, embedded in subtle details such as length of fur, viciousness of bark, and amount of gratuitous drool?

I had no choice. I closed myself off to the outside world for days, and read every Pleuss work from beginning to end.

Much has been written since his passing; many hurried and amateur attempts to explain Pleuss's work. I, unlike the others, have done my homework. I will admit that a few passages along the way were difficult to unravel, but I am confident that my intuition kept me on the mark.

I give you my findings....

The Green Mice, which Dr. Pleuss mentioned in his now-famous last words, were, as I'm sure every reader is aware, that band of ragtag odd-colored mice which appear in so many of his books, performing hi-jinx, concocting wacky schemes, and mourning the randomness of existence.

They first appeared in his early book, **Bunnies, Bunnies, Bunnies**, an interesting if immature effort, often criticized for failing to include bunnies in the story, after featuring them in the title. The Green Mice derive gleeful pleasure from terrorizing a town inhabited only by koala bears, showing some of the mischief they were later known for, but lacking the key characteristic that defined them in later works; their relentless hazing of opossums.

This early work shows some of Pleuss's later promise. Yet it comes across, all these years later, as an experimental effort by a young writer still finding his voice.

The book was popular enough when first released, though, and Pleuss followed its success with a very intense and productive period. Experts refer to this period as his "Green Phase." Pleuss himself had a turbulent relationship with his works from this period, and often referred to it as, "My goddamn green kick." We are referring, of course, to the titles of his three major works from this period; **The Green Turtle, The Green Llama,** and **The Green Thing With Little Sprockets on the side That Hurt A Lot if They Get Caught on Your Face**.

All three books were best sellers. Surprisingly, though, Pleuss neglected to include the Green Mice in any of these three books. When asked about it years later, Pleuss responded, "Didn't I? Hey, who stole my left pant leg?" This is a frustrating answer, but it may help explain the absence of certain minor plot points in these books, such as setting and story line.

Pleuss does, though, employ his first use of subtle hidden meaning in these books. Most strikingly, he seems to use the color green to expose man's reluctance to play the Sousa Phone in cramped quarters.

Also from this period is a little known departure piece, and Pleuss's first openly dark tale, titled, **Die, Entrée! Die!** Pleuss experiments here with more mature themes as he chronicles a man's futile attempts to cook his sushi. The story follows the man's obsession as it destroys first his mind, then his marriage, and ultimately the economy of Luxemburg. We are also treated to an appearance by the green mice in this book. They arrive near the end of the story, turning summersaults and bad mouthing existence.

His use of sushi in this tale reflects his childhood fear of seafood, a condition triggered at the age of seven when his cousin was allegedly hazed into embarrassment by a school of rebellious sturgeon.

Pleuss also deliberately referenced sturgeon during one gripping sequence (involving a suspenseful decision between a choice of side-dishes), subtly embedding a message, for those sensitive enough to perceive it, that not only are our rivers and streams dying, but that it is nearly impossible to water ski behind a canoe, an issue Pleuss felt strongly about, and returned to more than a few times.

The 'Green Phase' came to an abrupt end one day. Pleuss was reading to his young nephew. He was giving a heartfelt rendition of **The Green Llama** to the three year-old, and when he came to the end of the story the child stood up, went directly his brother's Lego model of a castle, and smashed it ruthlessly. Those who witnessed the scene say Pleuss quickly became distraught. He believed his story had caused this violence and that his stories were turning the world's children into monsters. He did not realize that the child was merely getting back at his brother for setting all his bed sheets on fire while he slept in them the night before. In fact, the child had shown amazing self-control, waiting until Pleuss finished the story before setting out on his vendetta.

Pleuss would not be comforted, though. He withdrew into moodiness and isolation. He could not write a word for months. When he finally did set pen to paper the result was a dark and ominous tale, titled, **The Hairball of Doom**, featuring a bizarre maroon colored creature with the head of a pterodactyl, the left wing of a mallard duck, and the right wing of a Boeing jet liner. It took me weeks of intense study to unravel the hidden meaning of this creature. After cross referencing and back-checking, I have come to the conclusion that it is a symbol for man's inability to cross a tightrope with an office chair strapped to his leg.

Hairball was not received well, by critics or readers. For the first time in his career, Dr. Pleuss received hate mail. This drove him into an even darker mood, resulting in his most pessimistic and bleak story, **The Goofy Bears Hear Voices Telling Them to Open a Leather Shop**.

This book seemed to purge the author of his bleak outlook, and his next two books marked a welcome return to playful and colorful settings. **One Fish, Two Fish, Red Fish, Mutant Beige Dog** sparkled with playfulness as it chronicled the education of a music lover who gets leprosy while chewing on a diesel engine, symbolizing, obviously, humanity's wastefulness, as well as one's need to wear pants at the zoo.

Pleuss then wrote **The Pythagorean Theorem And Ham**, a lasting masterpiece which details, with touching sentiment, his unfulfilled lifelong dream of playing bagpipes with the New York Philharmonic. The ultimate victory is won when, near the finale of Beethoven's Ninth, the Green Mice rise up from the brass section, quoting from the writings of St. Paul, declaring hope for the universe, and the entire orchestra is trotted off by a team of Huskies.

Throughout his career, Pleuss focused his sub textual themes on self-awareness, philosophical truth, and the magical power of lint balls. He only occasionally entered the political debate. His last book, **The Lemon Lime War**, was his most openly political. It was published just a few short months before his death. The war mentioned in the title is a loosely veiled reference to the often forgotten invasion of Lichtenstein by Moldova (to be fair, this was not so much an outright war, as it was a fight between several drunk men in a bar). His political stance, while obscured by a plot involving a candy manufacturer and some plaid sheep, seems to be a critical one. Pleuss seems to be saying either that the war was wrong, or that it was too lemony.

The book was received unenthusiastically by critics, but Pleuss's stature was such that most critics seemed reluctant to pan the book outright.

Pleuss seemed pleased with the book's commercial success, but suspected correctly that it as being misunderstood.

Three months after its publication, Pleuss fell ill. Doctors and nurses, dressed, as mentioned earlier, in rabbit suits (and a Priest nearby in a tuna costume) sustained him the best they could for a few weeks, but the great author's life had run its course.

In closing I leave you with the words of Pleuss's own Green Turtle, which I think sums it up about as well as anything can; "The road to happiness is narrow and fraught with danger, much like the road to Albuquerque, which is why you're advised to fly."

9
Why Is Love Always A Near-miss?
A short story, and sequel to *Movie Pizza Love*

Art began his walk by looking for the space that used to be The Last Exit.

That's where it all started. Art's older brother Doug had taken him there, how old was he 15? 13? Could it possibly have been 25, 26, 27 years ago?

This is the place, he realized, it's not a cafe at all anymore, it's actually a part of the University, The Learning Center, the sign said, this is the place, though, I am certain of it, he thought.

Had Art really been that teenager, enamored by his older brother and his intellectual friends and the chessboard tables and the whole idea of the University District? That was a lifetime ago, he thought. The University District and Art had changed so much, sometimes together, sometimes apart.

And here they stood. Art was preparing to say good bye to the U. District.

A block over - it's "Cafe Allegro at College Inn" now - used to be open 24 hours. Art had recently found an old journal entry he'd written there one night at the age of 20 or 21, staying up all night writing and drinking coffee and smoking - that was the one year he was a smoker - not because it was cool to stay up all night writing and drinking coffee and smoking, but because Art was homeless. Yes, Art had once been homeless, and the U. District was his home.

Downstairs is the College Inn Pub. Art was there two nights ago. Tess called him just as he was leaving, he stayed and waited to meet her. His best memory of the College Inn Pub was from a year and a half ago, was it really a year and a half ago, all his 20-something friends coming by to celebrate his 40th birthday? His most deeply held moment of the evening was when Tess showed up an approached his chair from behind, wrapping her arms around him. Later that evening she told him, "Art, all these people love you."

The best memories always involve Tess.

Art crossed Campus Parkway, leaving the College Inn behind, thinking about the three years - had it really been three years - since he and a 20-year-old Tess first danced together on the coffee table at that Garage House Halloween party. Tess is 23 now. He worked with her earlier today.

They're both leaving the pizza place later this week.

The memories of this neighborhood go back so many years, but life only goes on now, Art thought.

Cafe Solstice, where Lori used to work. Across the street, the Big Time Brewery and

Pub, Megan and Paul met me there, he remembered. Further up the block, Ave Copy Center, where he gets so much copy work done, whenever he walks in the guy says, "Hey, how are the screenplays doing?"

Across 42nd, Cafe On The Ave. Cafe On The Ave! That's Espresso Roma, what's this Cafe On The Ave business?

That's where he always had film people meet him. That's where he and The Actress met every Saturday earlier in the year, to talk about the film they would make in May and June.

Could you tell then what would happen, he wondered. Could you go back to those Saturday meetings in March and April and see any signs or warnings of what would happen?

Art stepped into Bulldog News to grab a Weekly and a Stranger, kept walking up the block. The electronics store where Mick used to work. Ruby, where Shawna is a bartender, Art and Tess and a few others closed the place one night last week. Flowers, Kai's, how many countless hours have I spent at Kai's, he wondered, as he crossed 43rd.

Four Corners Art and Frame. Art had bought cards there, cards he'd written in and given to Tess whenever she left town. It was a little ritual.

The Japanese store - what's it's name, anyway? University Bookstore, the heart and soul of the whole neighborhood. Across the street, Big 5 Sporting Goods, cheap shoes, the shoes he was wearing, the shoes that were falling apart on his feet. How many cheap pairs of shoes had he bought there?

Art waited to cross 45th. Coming up was the block they'd shot some of the film on. The guys on the street had begun calling him "The Actor." Now, months later, he was back to being just the Pizza Guy.

The Mix - they trade ice cream for pizza. The record store - going out of business. The space used to be Wizards Of The Coast. Art had worked in the restaurant there.

Across the street was the pizza place. So many people had left, so many were new. The new ones didn't have any idea he'd even shot a film there. In less than a week Art and Tess would be gone also.

Earlier today, working with her, he reminded himself to live up to what he had written about her.

Yes, they finally talked about that. I guess it's time to admit that I wrote about you a little, he said. She was not upset. For a year, he worried that she would be upset.

Art reflected on his own personal favorite moment with Tess. A month ago, after Carrie's going away party, they walked back from Wallingford with Sarah. Sarah walked ahead, and Art and Tess slipped behind, alone. She held his hand. You've left a permanent mark on me, he told her. And you've left a permanent mark on me, she said back.

Art kept walking up the block toward 47th. The Continental and Costas - where I -

Tommy's - Where Trent and I —

From 47th to 50th he was barely paying attention, lost in thought. Then he noticed the doorway to the stairs, the Halloween party from two weeks ago, the party where Sarah had said the thing that angered him. Art was talking about what a crazy year it had been; getting kicked out of the Garage House, making the movie, everyone leaving the pizza place. Then Art mentioned The Actress. Hey, you got laid, Sarah said in a cheery voice.

Art didn't find it funny.

Sunday night when Tess came to visit him at the other job, he sat down and vented about Sarah's comment.

So that's what it's reduced to? That month of turmoil, and the month afterwards when I was trying to figure out what happened? Is it all just reduced to getting laid?

For a Women's Studies graduate, Sarah sure has a frat-boy mentality, Art said.

And what did happen, anyway, Art wondered. It wasn't just sleeping-with-the-actress. It wasn't some sordid cheap thing. It was a relationship, or an attempt at one, anyway. Maybe it was a failed attempt, but a serious one.

And maybe he can never have a relationship as long as Tess has so much of his heart.

Crossing 50th he reminded himself, I'm too old for her, or too...boring. Or too SOMETHING.

He remembered the time he sent Tess a message. He knew she didn't check her messages often, so he called her to tell her. I sent you a message, he said. It's a question.

What's the question, she asked.

You have to read it, he said.

What's the question?

I can't tell you over the phone, he said.

Maybe when I'm 30, if I'm not married, she said jokingly.

No, he said laughing. That's not the question.

Why is love always a near-miss, Art wondered, crossing 52nd. In soccer, if you have ten near-misses, you eventually put one shot on target. Have I had ten near-misses yet? Who can even keep track of something like that?

The Galway Arms, where Liza used to play. That's who he had based that part of the Actresses character on.

How bizarrely connected everything is. Liza was an Extra in the other film. She was a singer-songwriter - she lived with Art for a while. He moved out of that apartment, moved into the Garage House, eventually moved back to an apartment across the courtyard from the first one, made this new movie, with The Actress, who is a singer-songwriter, and who lived with Art for a time.

But the emotional content of the character was Tess, not Liza. And The Actress. The Actress made it her own, so let's not lose our grip, Art reminded himself. The movie is The Actresses, not someone else's.

Crossing 55th - Pizza Pi - used to be the delivery kitchen Art worked at. Walking past he noticed the ovens - the two we left them, Art thought, we had four in there, took two, left two.

University Theater, where they shot the end of the movie.

Past 56th.

Home.

It's Freddie's 21st tonight. Another one of my friends is turning 21, Art thought. Is it too much to ask that all of my friends at least be over 21?

There are still one or two who aren't.

The Actress called Freddie The Sloppy guy.

It's good to have friends.

Tess will be there.

Part Two:
Simple Displeasures

10
Cheney Emails Declassified

Ten years after the fact, the CIA has declassified documents from the first years of the Bush-Cheney Administration.

While our researchers are still going through the many documents, looking for an actual news item, we came across these emails from the former Vice President, and found them interesting.

March 12, 2001

To All White House Staff: Whoever has been eating my Jolly Ranchers is going to die.

March 14, 2001

To All White House Staff: Listen clowns, you have to stop telling jokes in the hallways about my heart attacks. I am listening to everything!

In case you missed the earlier memo, we are calling them "Heart Attacks" so the public does not get confused. In fact, what is happening is that my micro-cell power pack is running low. It makes me twitchy.

March 16, 2001

Attached is a list of staff members I would like to invite on my next hunting trip (Fun! Yeah!?) [attachment missing from CIA files]

March 17, 2001

In Case of Emergency:

Hi everyone; my inventor - I mean "Doctor" - has informed me that I need to give all key staff members the following instructions, should I suffer a serious "heart attack" in your presence. Since I do not technically have a "heart" in the strictest sense of the word, please do not panic. Simply follow these instructions, and everything will be fine.

1. At the top of my back, just below the neck, is a small panel. Press the red button, and a door will open on my chest.

2. Inside my chest you will find three plug-in jacks. Use a normal, everyday extension cord. Plug one end into a near-by wall socket, and attach the other end to the red

jack in my chest.

Re-charging should take about an hour. Please do not make me do any interviews, or talk to the media, until fully charged.

April 7, 2001

To All White House Staff: Very Funny! Ha ha! Tee freakin' Hee! Did I mention that I am listening to everything!? So, Bob, David, Sam, Lisa, you are all going hunting with me next week. Non-negotiable. And you're going to enjoy it, whether you want to or not.

I'm excited! Getting twitchy just thinking about it.

11
Sexy Girls on Motorcycles

There are certain things about a person, about me anyway, that have to be explained over and over. I don't want to keep explaining these things, but they keep coming up.

It happened again recently with the issue of girls, sexiness, and motorcycles.

I SHOULD think motorcycles are cool. I SHOULD love the ethos of individuality, travel, and power that a motorcycle represents.

I SHOULD think there is nothing sexier than a sexy girl on a motorcycle.

Certain events mark a person's life, though. There is nothing we can do about certain happenings. They stay with us.

I don't remember exactly how old I was, maybe seven or eight.

We lived about 40 miles outside of Seattle. It was the "country" more or less. We were on 2 acres. The neighbors had 5. An entire 10-acre neighboring stretch had maybe 4 houses on it.

My brother Dan, a couple years older than me, was friends with Mark, who lived in one of the houses down a dirt road. Mark was also older, and I tagged along after them, just wishing I could be as cool as they were.

That's your perspective on the world when you're the youngest of a group.

Mark owned a mini-bike - a small motorized machine that he would buzz around on. Living with so much open space invited it. The fact that he owned and rode what was basically a miniature motorcycle at such a young age made him the coolest person in the world, I thought. I thought this until he and Dan goaded me into sitting on the damn thing myself.

Mark had created a jump. It was simple, a tilted piece of plywood, rising from ground-level to a height of maybe 3 feet.

Mark and Dan took turns jumping off it. They would rev up the bike, speed toward the plywood ramp, and fly off the high end into the air.

They actually took flight. More surprisingly, though, they always managed to land perfectly.

It looked fun.

Deep down I knew that it was the sort of fun that I should just watch, not participate in. But older brothers and older friends have their own ideas, and they wouldn't take no for an answer.

I protested as forcefully as I could, but I was powerless.

Suddenly there I was, on the bike, throttle in my right hand. I had no idea how to use the brake.

The thing took off, faster than I could control. Steering it at all was a crap-shoot.

I was arriving at the plywood ramp at the wrong angle. I hit the bottom of the ramp in a panic.

The front wheel lurched to the left.

I drove - tumbled, really - off the side of the ramp, wheel first, into the grass.

I had no control, and no idea what was happening.

All I remember is grass and wheels and an engine on top of me and a screaming sound that seemed to be coming from ME.

I scrambled to my feet and ran. I just ran.

I had to get away as far and as fast as I could.

I heard someone yelling. It might have been Mark yelling after me about what I had just done to his bike.

I didn't care. All I cared about was distance. I had to be as far away from that machine as possible.

So...I apologize.

I apologize to an ex-girlfriend, and to what might have been a maybe would-be girlfriend (I can never be sure of these things) who were sure they would wow me with their sexiness on a motorcycle.

It was probably true...You are sexy on a motorcycle.

I just can't be around that. And yes, I agree, I am certainly missing out.

12

Gay Divorce

Note: this piece was written prior to the Supreme Court's landmark 2015 ruling legalizing gay marriage nation-wide)

I have a few friends who have marched in the street over the issue of gay marriage.

When California's Proposition 8 banned gay marriage in the state, one friend in particular – a straight female – joined a crowd of people who shut down Santa Monica Boulevard in Los Angeles.

When she asked me why I didn't join the march, I said, "I've been married...and divorced. I don't see myself spending a lot of my time and energy supporting marriage. Divorce? Maybe."

So, when I read this past week that a lesbian couple, married two years ago in the state of Maryland, were having trouble getting a divorce, I decided it was time to rise up and join the cause.

My position is a simple one; divorce is a right that no one should be denied. Divorce is one of the great gifts bestowed on us either by a divine creator or, if he doesn't exist, at least by a divorce court judge. It is a gift of importance and great magnitude. No one, regardless of their sexual orientation, should be denied the right to get the hell out of a dysfunctional relationship.

Those who say divorce should only be between one man and one woman, have obviously never heard my gay neighbors arguing at 3 in the morning. Technically they are not married, but they sure act like an old married couple.

All of us are created equal. None of us should be denied the right to STAY in a bad relationship if we want to. None of us should be denied the right to be bored with our partner of 12 years – the inalienable right to go out to dinner out of sheer boredom, to sit numbly over your food brooding over the fact that you've had nothing to say to each other since 2004.

So also should none of us be denied the right to passive-aggressively jab at each other with snarky zingers until the divorce lawyers intervene and try to keep things at least moderately civil.

In short, this lesbian couple must be granted their divorce, and quickly, before expensive plates get broken.

It is the humanitarian thing to do.

Step up to the plate, Maryland.

Grant the divorce.

Do not allow prejudice over sexual orientation to cloud your judgment.
Let these two miserable ex's walk away from each other, for cryin' out loud.

13
The Guy Who Saves String

The guy who saves string...A crazy invention from the mind of Woody Allen, from the short pieces he published years ago.

The guy who saves string shuffles oddly down the street, mumbling to himself, obsessing over string, how to save it, and how he can find more of it.

It is one of those mental images that makes a you laugh the first time you read about it, and nearly every time it pops into your thoughts from then on.

So...when I began unpacking a 15-year-old box from my storage space, and pulled from among the stacks of useless old papers, a single piece of string, I realized I had some self-examining to do.

Technically it's bigger than string. It's either a very long shoe lace, or the kind of lace you tie swim trunks around your waist with. But let's be honest; it's string...and I saved it...in a box...for 15 years.

There are many different reason for saving things:

-Reminders of important events in your life.

-Ideas jotted down that you might someday carry out.

-Things that once influenced or helped shape who you have become.

This is a piece of string, though. The only reason I can come up with that might explain why I saved it, is that I was convinced that sometime in the distant future something might desperately need to be tied up.

That doesn't help me much.

I want to go into denial about this.

There are other things in this box from 15 years ago that I can't explain:

-Empty envelopes...

Apparently, on several occasions, I received something in the mail, opened the envelope, took out the contents, and saved the empty envelope.

And it isn't as if I opened it carefully, planning to re-use the empty envelope. No, I tore the damn thing open...then saved it.

-A Tennis magazine, with Yannik Noah on the cover.

At least that is slightly interesting today, since I have been watching his son Joakim play basketball in the NBA.

That helps a little.

Sometimes you save something on gut instinct; Maybe, just maybe, this magazine with this tennis player on the cover will resonate in some unique way in the future.

I suppose I was thinking the piece of string would resonate in some unique way someday; "Oh yeah, remember that time when we had the string, and we used it to… to um….tie that….that thing….to the other thing….you know with this piece of string?" "Yeah, that was awesome."

Nope. I have LOTS of self-examining to do.

And don't even get me started on the expired old driver's license of an ex-girlfriend…

14
Violence

(Note: The following piece is depressing and serious. It recalls a real event, one of violence that I was personally connected to. While considering whether to include it in this collection, I realized that so many people have experienced similar violent situations in their own lives, that I felt a need to include it here, in solidarity with everyone who has their own similar story. It refers to the "Café Racer shooting" of May, 2012. – P.W.)

I hung out with some relatively new friends last Friday night; drinks at a bar on Venice Beach, California; a healthy dose of happy drunkenness (less by me than by a girl who, for her sake and mine, I will call 'Mary'), a late-night run onto the beach itself...it was a celebration of life...Life...in its simplest form, fun, wondrous, mysterious, but mostly just fun.

It took my mind off the events of 2 weeks earlier.

A little more than a year ago, during the first handful of months of 2011, I was in a Seattle stretch of what was basically a 5-year-long Seattle-Los Angeles split of my time.

I became a semi-regular, during those months, at a little cafe and bar a block from where I lived, called CAFE RACER.

I call myself a 'semi-regular' because, compared to the real 'regulars,' I was a pretender. There were several good people who almost seemed to live there.

I made a point of showing up when Amy was bartending - and not just because she seemed to erase a drink or 2 from my tab at the end of the night. I would arrive at 7 or 8 in the evening as Len, the Chef, was closing the kitchen.

I really just wanted to hang out with Amy, but she was working, so when Len would pull up a bar stool and settle into his post-shift beer, we struck up a comfortable friendship.

Len is a good guy, quit a computer job to go to culinary school. I overheard him once telling Kurt, the owner of Cafe Racer, that he had been looking on Craigslist for Chef positions in Hawaii.

Two weeks ago, on Wednesday, May 30th, about 5pm, I received the first of several messages from friends in Seattle.

A mentally ill gunman who had been kicked out of Cafe Racer for being obnoxious and disorderly, came back and shot 5 people.

Len took 2 bullets, luckily missing his spine and vital organs.

Bleeding, he called 911. The mentally ill gunman later took his own life.

Things were confusing that night. No one had all the names of the victims. I had to ask Amy, via text message, the very unusual question, "Hey, you haven't been shot have you." I sent the message as the horrifying thought crossed my mind, what if I never hear back? Thankfully she replied. She wasn't there when it happened.

This is difficult to write about, but I am doing it because it happened. There is no escape from this fact.

I am also writing about it because it only took 3 days for a different shooting in a different city to replace it in the headlines.

First there was a mall shooting in Toronto. This week it was 3 dead at Auburn University...and 4 more in Sacramento.

As I write this Len is still in the hospital, but doing well. He is the survivor of the Cafe Racer shooting. 4 others are dead.

So many thoughts cross my mind as I sit writing - don't get too preachy (the mentally ill gunman had a concealed weapons permit), don't get too maudlin (real people deal with real tragedies every day somewhere in this world), don't be too selfish (the two people who I knew the best at Café Racer are alive).

In the end I just come away with a renewed sense that guns matter.

I have grown tired of going to movies where people are shot for sport (just about every action blockbuster ever made). I am relieved when guns are portrayed with some sense of their real impact (check out the D-Day scene that opens Spielberg's "Saving Private Ryan" again).

In the end I have no real insights, no solutions. I guess it is worthwhile to remember - in the midst of all our planning and ambition and focusing on the future - that right now might be your whole life. Celebrate it.

Go for a late night run on a beach somewhere.

And think about Len...and his surprising but welcome recovery.

15

Democrats, Republicans, and Aliens from Outer Space
(Written during the MUCH SIMPLER TIME of the 2012 Presidential election)

I have been surprised to come across, not one, but two important news items involving Aliens from outer space recently.

First, reported by Jon Stewart on The Daily Show, a recent Presidential poll found that Barack Obama is leading Mitt Romney by a staggering 65% to 35% when respondents were asked who they trusted more to deal with an invasion by space Aliens.

Now, you might be tempted to think this was a joke. I certainly did, until I read another story, in which an ex-CIA Agent confirmed that the Roswell, New Mexico incident of 1947 was in fact a crashed Alien space craft, and included dead Alien bodies.

This could turn the year's coming election on its head...but not in the way you might think.

In 2008, the prestigious journal, National Enquirer, reported that Barack Obama had wrapped up important support from space Aliens during his primary battle against Hilary Clinton.

Why? Why would the space Alien politicos back Obama? Had Bill Clinton squandered his Alien support while he was President?

And if Obama has the support of extra-terrestrials, can we really trust him to handle the coming invasion?

This is not to suggest that Mitt Romney would be better. I agree with the 65% who do not trust Mitt Romney to respond adequately when staring down Alien photon torpedoes.

So, what are we to make of all this? Are we trapped? Are we doomed to re-elect a President who may already be in cahoots with those about to invade us from space? Is our only option this starched technocrat who will probably be anti-space-alien only until it helps his career to become pro-space-alien?

These are rhetorical questions, dear readers. I do not have the answers.

The game may already be over.

Does anyone know how Ron Paul feels about space aliens?

Hm? He IS one?

Figures...

Dennis Kucinich?

Never mind.

16

Curiosity

I don't want to sound like too much of a nerd.

I mean, I'm NOT a nerd, am I? I play soccer every Saturday. I've been talking football with some friends since the new NFL season started.

I AM NOT A NERD!

But really....I sort of am one.

I have fallen totally and completely in love with a robot.

When I last wrote in this space, two months ago, it was a silly little thing about aliens from outer space. Since I wrote it, NASA has landed one of the most amazing pieces of machinery -The Curiosity Rover - on Mars. The machine is driving around our neighboring planet, taking pictures.

Curiosity has more charisma, to me, than a Movie Star. It flew thousands of miles through space, dropped onto an alien planet, and just started driving around.

The pictures - bleak, barren, empty - are absolutely stunning to me.

When I look out my bedroom window now, at the view of distant mountains circling the north and east of Los Angeles, I no longer see Los Angeles, or California, or even the United States of America. That's too small.

I see Planet Earth, hurtling through space around a hot burning ball. We are all along for the ride, with absolutely no control over our destiny.

It wouldn't take much to snuff out our entire species, to crush our little cosmic bus. It has happened to bigger balls in space.

And now we have visited another ball.

There isn't much there. No plants, no creatures. Maybe there is some water, or ice. Maybe a few of us will visit in a decade or two or three.

I find the whole adventure invigorating.

It is a welcome distraction from the small problems we take so seriously on this little ball; who will be the next President of one of our little pieces of land; will the next little gadget be faster than the last one?

I was reading an article recently that described the next iPhone as "technology."

No, I said, almost out loud. That's not technology. That's a gadget.

"Curiosity" is technology.

I have been re-reading Ray Bradbury's "The Martian Chronicles." I had to pick it up again, especially after NASA named the spot where Curiosity landed, "Bradbury Landing."

Visiting the NASA website, I also looked up the Cassini Probe, which has been flying around a pretty big ball, Saturn, for eight years now. It is telling us a lot about a very interesting smaller ball, Saturn's moon Titan, which may have a sub-surface water ocean.

It makes you realize that all the little squabbles between us and our brothers and sisters (all the other human beings who may or may not look different from us) are really quite petty and small-minded.

So someone believes some religion or other. Someone hates someone else. Some country thinks they are the best country ever.

As a species, I think we need to just get over ourselves.

Quit arguing about who deserves the best seat on the cosmic bus, settle in with our family of 7 billion brothers and sisters, and enjoy the ride.

17
Free Pussy Riot
(Written in 2012, with a follow-up note at the end)

According to several aging Russian hippies, bootlegged copies of The Beatles music had as much to do with the downfall of the Soviet Union as any politician or political movement.

The songs of the Beatles - banned by the Soviet leadership in the 1960's - permeated an underground Russian youth culture so thoroughly, that by the time that generation reached maturity in the 1980's, a majority of Russian society had little or no stomach left for Soviet ideology.

They were over it. Art - in the form of music - had enlightened them in ways beyond what even John, Paul, George, or Ringo could have intended.

Art and creativity can do that. It can change the way entire generations think.

The Soviet Union' is a historical relic now. In its place are Russia, Ukraine, Latvia, Lithuania, and several other smaller independent countries.

Russia is currently ruled by one Vladimir Putin, and his hold on power is so absolute that you can be arrested for criticizing his policies.

This is what happened to performance-art-feminist-punk-band Pussy Riot.

In February, earlier this year, they staged what has been called a flash-mob-style invasion of a Russian Orthodox Church and performed their "Punk Prayer," before being arrested.

They have been found guilty of disrupting public order, and hooliganism (I thought you had to be involved in a drunken fight outside a soccer game to be convicted of hooliganism). Two of the band members have managed to flee the country, and one saw her conviction dropped (because she was actually arrested BEFORE she had a chance to perform the offending song). Two members of Pussy Riot remain in prison, sent to what are described as 'penal colonies.'

I and many of my friends identify, in one discipline or another, as "Artists." For the most part we only have to worry about superficial things; am I making a living at this or do I have to get a day job? Will I get the Million-dollar contract or do I have to settle for something smaller?

It's easy to lose sight of deeper issues.

There are no more courageous Artists in this world right now than the five members of Pussy Riot.

Earlier today I joined Amnesty International. I had been thinking about it for some time.

The recent Presidential campaigns in the U.S. left me feeling a little, shall we say, UNDERNOURISHED, regarding the issues that actually seem to matter.

But this is not about living in one country as opposed to another. We are a planetary family. What happens to an Artist in Russia affects us all.

(The jailed members of Pussy Riot were released prior to the 2014 Sochi Winter Olympics in Russia. They criticized their own release as a publicity stunt to make Russia look better before to the Olympics. They are continuing to stir things up with creative, unexpected, daring performances. ROCK ON, Pussy Riot!)

18
Bob Dylan's Dentist

Living in Los Angeles comes with its own unique brand of surprises.

You never know where the latest bizarre celebrity story is going to come from.

I was sitting in a dentist chair recently, leaning back the way only a dentist chair car force you to lean back. I was looking up at the ceiling waiting for the dentist to begin poking around in my mouth, when I overheard a conversation about Bob Dylan's teeth.

The two dentists in the office were ignoring me. They were talking about their favorite music. They seemed to agree on classic rock. I felt a strong impulse to jump into the conversation and suggest that classic rock is great, but try giving something more recent a fighting chance; the grunge era perhaps, or hip hop from the early 2000's (pre-Jimmy-Fallon era Roots, Talib Kweli, Jurassic 5). I stayed silent, though.

As I listened, I realized that dentists have a different take, even on music, than the rest of us.

One of the dentists, it turns out, has a colleague in town who pokes around inside Bob Dylan's mouth.

"Oh, the stories," the first dentist said.

"Yeah?"

"Bob Dylan comes in with his 'handler,' head down. He never looks you in the eye. Apparently he is completely unable to communicate on any kind of normal level."

"Really! huh," said the second dentist

I lost interest when they started talking about Bob Dylan's periodontal issues.

I wish I had not overheard the story.

On one level I am always aware that celebrities are real, living breathing people, with the same physical limitations as the rest of us, but somehow it feels slightly wrong to listen to, say, "Knocking on Heaven's Door," and suddenly become overwhelmed with concern about the man's gums.

I suppose that's better than listening to the cover version by Guns And Roses, though.

Somehow I just assume Axel Rose's mouth is a disaster area.

Next up? I have to schedule an eye appointment. I don't have a regular eye Doctor in Los Angeles, so I'm free to try somewhere new.

Where will I likely hear stories about Johnny Depp? I just have a feeling that guy's as blind as a bat.

19

To Brit or Not to Brit

For as long as I can remember, I have struggled with conflicting emotions about the British DNA coursing through my blood.

Through different branches of my Mother's ancestry, my family is from two different parts of England; Dover in the south, and York, in the middle.

Battling these ancestral branches are a Scottish branch and German one. Come to think of it, maybe it was the Scots and the Germans who separately moved from their own countries to York. Anyway, they all eventually left England for America, and here we are.

On my Father's side was his Father, a seafaring Norwegian who, by himself at 18, took a ship from Norway to Liverpool, England, another ship across the ocean to Montreal, a train across the American continent to Seattle, and within a couple months was in Alaska on a fishing boat.

My Father's Mother was also from Norway, but when she researched her own ancestry, became embarrassingly distraught to discover a Jewish branch of the family.

For the record I want to reconcile my Grandmother's WASP and Jewish mixture. I embrace it...Mazel Tov!

The reason I am writing this, though, is to try to put my maternal British heritage into some sort of perspective.

As someone prone toward the creative arts, I have sometimes felt a strong identification with my British DNA.

Shakespeare wrote my favorite piece of writing. Charlie Dickens knocked off a few good yarns. And I would rather watch a British detective show than an American one any day of the week.

These pro-Brit feelings are on one side of the coin. On the other side - and this is where the problems arise - must be the Scottish part of me, unable to shake the "Trainspotting" line about Brits being 'wankers.'

Or maybe it is just my rebellious American side.

Several years ago, when my sister was studying at Leeds University in England, we began corresponding about the discovery that we apparently qualified for a British Coat-of-Arms.

It was fun for a while. We brainstormed and discussed Coat-of-Arms themes (a family of teachers, writers, and amateur athletes ought to inspire some interesting design ideas). Then something happened inside of me. Deep in the middle of this process of pursuing a British Coat-of-Arms, I woke up one morning and said, "You know what, screw the British! Screw their pretentious Coat-of-Arms bullshit." And the idea died as quickly as it had been born.

So, now I ask myself, what's it going to be? Do I embrace the legacy of literature, theater, and culture? Or do I reject the questionable legacy of Empire, exploitation, and unintended political comedy? (And someone please tell me - what is the point of a 'royal family' in the 21st century?)

The only British politicians I have ever had any respect for were characters portrayed by Monty Python.

So, if someone can tell me who is currently the head of the Ministry Of Silly Walks, then maybe we have something to talk about.

20
I Am Not a Bank Robber

It's been a few years, but for some reason I kept the three business cards in my wallet.

The business cards are; Officer Brian Thomas, Seattle Police Department, Lieutenant Peter J. Celms of the University of Washington Police, and Patrol Sergeant T. Prat-Wieberg, also of the UW Police.

It had started like any other day. I was walking casually down Roosevelt in Seattle's University District, lost in thought (I am always lost in thought, sometimes I appear to be lost in thought when I am actually only half-awake, but the two states are similar enough that I maintain my claim that I am always lost in thought).

As I walked into the Fedex Office store on 45th I noticed a Police car pulling up behind me. Then another Police car. Then two more.

An officer pushed the Fedex door open and said, "Excuse me, sir, please step outside."

Unsure who they were talking to, I paid no attention and stepped up to a self-serve copy machine.

"Sir! You! Please step outside now!"

I looked in the direction of the voice and realized that several cops were staring directly at me. I twisted my face sideways, trying to process what was happening, and stepped toward them.

"Hands out of your pockets!" the officer yelled. "What's in your pocket? Remove your hand slowly!"

"Yeah," I said, sarcasm creeping into my voice, "It's papers. I don't think they're loaded."

None of the cops seemed to appreciate the sarcasm. This was difficult to accept. As a sometimes-stand-up-comedian, I am always reading those around me to see whether something is going over well. This was not going over well.

At this point in the story I should point out - for those who don't really know me - that I can be a little, well, let's call it 'mouthy' at times. I can talk my way into trouble. Sometimes words, attitude, just sort of slip out.

"What did I do?" I asked innocently enough, until I followed it with, "Was it something cool? I'd like to know."

"We'll be asking the questions," the officer said.

"No," I said, "actually I'll be asking lots of questions too."

"Up against the wall!"

The officer began patting me down, and asked me to empty my pockets slowly. It was at this point that I noticed that several of the officers were UW Police, a sorry band of misfits, in training with the County Sherriff's Department. I tried to hold back the comment, but I couldn't. It spilled out of my mouth before I could catch it.

"Oh my god," I said, "you're not even a real cop!"

A moment of what you can only call 'tension' followed, as several officers battled their urge to attack me.

Finally the lead officer (a 'real' cop) got off his walkie talkie and apologized to me. I did not match the description of the bank robber as closely as first thought. The officer explained to me that they were looking for a man with brown hair, blue jeans, and a white jacket.

"Hey, maybe you shouldn't have wasted all your time on a guy with blond hair, sweats, and a grey jacket," I said.

An awkward silence followed.

I looked at the army of police cars circling me, and the ten or so officers.

"Maybe some of you should have gone up these alleys looking for the guy," I said. "He's probably gotten away by now."

And as the officers surrounding me fought mightily with their own urges to pummel me into small pieces, I realized that now might be a good time to stop talking.

If I had said anything more, a crime would have happened that day, and the person who committed the crime would have gotten away with it, because those with him would have backed him up. Of course I would never know the outcome of the case. I would have been beaten senseless by fake officers coming at me from all directions.

21
Places on Earth

I live in Los Angeles year-round now. So I have grudgingly accepted that my occasional visits home to Seattle now happen by airplane.

It took five years, but I eventually burned out on the 2-day drive up or down the coast. I did it at least twice a year from 2007 to 2012, when I more or less split my time between the two cities. The drive can be quicker than two days, but when I did it, I stopped too often, shutting off the car to stare out at nature.

There are places along the coast of northern California and southern Oregon where the beauty defies words or descriptions. You have to just stop the car, get out, walk along the beach, take it in as fully as you can, then get back in the car and go, a slightly changed person.

I miss these places.

I have been to lots of places on this little ball we live on. Friends of mine have been to many more places than me, but I've been around a little.

Here in the United States I've been to most of the major cities; New York a few times, Chicago, Denver, Dallas, Houston, Miami, Minneapolis, Indianapolis, Cleveland, Washington, D.C.

I lived in San Francisco for three months when I was 18, attending a small college that left town shortly after I left the college.

I lived in Phoenix, Arizona for a year when I was too young to remember it. I know Phoenix mostly from summer visits through the rest of my childhood.

I've been to London and Paris, but I have often joked about the fact that while in Paris I ate at McDonald's one day. Some of my friends believe that eating at McDonald's in Paris more or less cancels the trip; you didn't really go.

I have also been to Munich, Germany, Vancouver, Canada, and parts of Mexico and Switzerland.

I have camped in a tent in the woods, and looked down at Times Square from many floors up in a Manhattan hotel room.

Why do I mention all this?

I've been thinking about our little ball-in-space recently. I like our little ball. It's the right distance from the sun. It has amazing oceans, mountains, deserts, and swamps.

I have never been to Asia, but I read, just this morning, that more than 2 million deaths are caused each year - the majority of them in Asia - by air pollution.

I also read on the NASA website that warming oceans are causing what they called "basal melting;" ice melting underneath the Antarctic ice shelf.

Environmental science is a complex thing, and I do not want to over-simplify things here.

Since I visited the Florida Everglades for the first time this past April, I have been reading up on the science of Everglades devastation and attempted restoration. It's a depressing read.

Two of my friends this weekend are sitting in boats on a lake in Mammoth, California. They are fishing.

I'm jealous of them. I want to be on a boat fishing, far away from these sounds of L.A. traffic outside my window.

Not everyone agrees on issues of pollution, the environment we live in, or the health of our little ball-in-space. And certainly not everyone agrees on how things ought to change going forward.

It is my hope, though, that we can all begin to agree on some basic truths:

-A lake in Mammoth, California, filled with fish, is a beautiful thing.

-The Pacific Ocean, viewed from a cold Oregon beach in October is a beautiful thing.

-An alligator staring up at you from half-submerged eyes, in the Florida Everglades, is a beautiful thing.

This ball we live on is actually pretty small. You can fly all the way around it making only two or three stops. You can orbit it in the Space Station in about an hour and a half.

We have changed our planet. We have to accept that at this point. Welcome to the new reality.

Maybe we can agree that the driving principle going forward should be based on a little bit of love for our fragile little ball-in-space.

Just a thought.

22

The Peacefulness of the Un-governed

(Written in October, 2013, during a government shutdown due to conflict between Republicans and Democrats)

I have no desire to write a political editorial.

As I write this, though, our government is shut down, and has been for a couple weeks.

While everyone else is clamoring to score points with one argument or another, blaming Republicans, blaming Democrats, I prefer to sit quietly, watch the sunset, and feel the unusual calm of being un-governed.

I have often described my political views by quoting the line from the Groucho Marx song; "Whatever it is, I'm against it."

I think it's a reasonable position to take. It may be the only reasonable position to take on the politics of 2013.

This in no way makes me a Libertarian. I am as firmly against Libertarians as I am against all politicians.

The government shutdown means that food inspectors are furloughed. Scientists are not getting paid. National Parks are closed. Secret surveillance of our private phone calls has been interrupted.

This is a funny feeling, this state of being un-governed. It's something everyone should experience for a few weeks of their life.

I was reading, this past weekend, about several car-makers' intense desire to manufacture and sell self-driving cars within the next decade.

These cars will deal with traffic, stop for pedestrians, and take you wherever you want to go, all while you sit back and play games on your phone.

The stickiest problem these car makers have to solve is; who is responsible when the self-driving car malfunctions, runs up on the sidewalk, and causes carnage when it fails to stop at a red light?

The government is getting in on the act. Government regulators will have to determine the safety standards before these machines can take to the road.

The standards will be extremely high. Government safety inspectors are funny people. They don't care what your politics are. They just take safety very seriously.

I think about this whenever I board an airplane. I trust the safety inspectors to have checked my plane thoroughly.

I don't much like government. I don't think the political process should be taken at all seriously, and politicians should always be viewed with suspicion, like mobsters, or salesmen, or CEO's.

So, I am enjoying being un-governed.

Whatever it is, I'm against it.

But I am also against the government being shut down for too much longer.

Being un-governed truly is a peaceful feeling.

It's like that peaceful feeling you have in the airplane, right at that moment you have accepted what's about to happen, seconds before the airplane crashes into the side of the mountain.

23
The Middle of Somewhere

I was back home in Seattle over the recent holidays, feeling completely at home and comfortable. I enjoyed the company of friends who I miss, and family who are a part of me.

It didn't feel like a year since my last visit, and I found myself promising a few friends that I would make it back a few times during the coming year.

Seattle is home. L.A. is home. These places I am familiar with.

I found myself thinking, though, about places that I've visited that are definitely not home.

My thoughts traveled back in time to a week of my life that began in Decatur, Illinois and ended in Appleton, Wisconsin.

I was in my 20's and was working a stand-up comedy tour of small-town Midwest clubs. I use the word 'clubs' loosely.

The week started on Tuesday, with me driving a rental car south from Chicago into small-town Illinois, for what is still the only time of my life.

Tuesday night's gig was a one-nighter in Decatur. I arrived at the 'club' which was a small local tavern, where the regulars merely tolerated the once-a-week invasion by two stand-up comedians. I was the opening act, and I apologize to whoever followed me; I have no memory of who was loosely referred to as the 'headliner.'

My only memory of Decatur, Illinois is this tavern.

It didn't have a stage.

To perform I had to climb up onto two tables that had been placed next to each other. I did my best to get and keep the audience's attention, but I lost the battle to the Chicago Cubs. The biggest laugh of the whole night came when I gave up, dropped the microphone, and turned to watch the Cubs with them.

The next night was Rockford, Illinois, and then Thursday, Friday, and Saturday were in Appleton, Wisconsin.

I am happy to report that the gigs gradually improved through the week. Appleton was good to me.

The most striking memory of the week for me, though, was the driving; driving through Wisconsin farm country in the summertime. It was beautiful.

It remains a vision that I can't seem to shake years later.

Sometimes those of us who live in a big city like Los Angeles (or New York or London or Paris or Tokyo or Shanghai) find ourselves feeling a little cocky about being in the middle of something; the eye of the storm; where the action is.

I like to remember another kind of middle; the middle of nowhere - which is really always somewhere.

I have to drive through small-town Illinois, and Wisconsin again sometime.

I plan to get out of the car at some small tavern, maybe on a weeknight when a little entertainment might be passing through town.

I plan to sit and have a beer and make a couple of local friends. I plan to celebrate life in the middle of somewhere.

24

Brothers

I'm not sure what year it was. I think I was in First or Second grade. My brother David would have been in Junior High School. He had received a Daisy air rifle BB gun as a Christmas present and promptly spent the following week shooting tree trunks, blades of grass, basically declaring war on all inanimate objects in the neighborhood.

He became bored with these lifeless enemies, though, so he decided to move on to the most logical next target; our other brother Dan.

Dan is the middle brother; older than me, younger than David.

Anyone who has either been a part of, observed, or even come across a family with three brothers, knows that this is a very dangerous situation, one that is on the verge of combustion at any given time.

Brothers - especially when there are three of them - have a tendency to hurt each other for fun, injure each other for laughs, insult each other as a way to simply pass the time.

David lay on his stomach on the floor of the bedroom.

He was mostly hidden behind the doorway. He aimed the air rifle carefully at Dan, who was vacuuming the living room, a chore my mother had placed on him.

To me David looked like the perfect sniper hiding in the grass, sizing up his unsuspecting victim.

I was behind David and I was absolutely beside myself. I was jumping up and down with an uncontrollable mix of excitement and fear.

"Sh! Quiet!" David whispered back at me.

"Do it! Do it!" I whispered back.

David lay his cheek down carefully on the butt of the gun. He adjusted his eye onto the site and took a slow breath.

Dan was turned away from us, pushing and pulling the vacuum cleaner on the carpet. He was wearing blue jeans, his butt a worthy and inviting target.

The suspense was killing me.

POP!

David pulled the trigger.

The wail that came from Dan's mouth was a thing of terrifying beauty.

It pierced that wall of vacuum-cleaner noise and must certainly have travelled out into the street, to the neighbor's houses.

He twisted to look down at his own butt, where a clear indentation the size of a tiny BB showed in his blue jeans. The BB itself had fallen harmlessly to the floor.

My mother came rushing into the room, as David and I quickly hid inside the bedroom, sharing hysterical laughter.

Our laughter gave us away. My mom and Dan came into the room and looked at us.

"Did you shoot your brother with the BB gun?"

We tried to hold our laughter, but couldn't. We were cracking up uncontrollably.

Even Dan, who was settling into the knowledge that his jeans had prevented any real injury, was beginning to smile a little.

"Listen," my mom said, "there's no shooting people. You don't shoot your brother in the house. Do you hear me? No shooting your brother in the house."

I guess it was a reasonable new ground rule to lay down.

It was too late, though. The moment had already happened, and a moment like that lasts forever.

25
Chris Farley

When Chris Farley's "Down by the river" sketch was named greatest SNL sketch of all time recently, I was reminded of the one time I met Chris Farley.

I should probably say up front that telling this story is not intended to be any kind of definitive statement about who Chris Farley was or what he was like. This is the only time I ever met him. Someone who knew him better than me would have to put this story into perspective.

It was 1993, during a year-and-a-half-long period in which I took any small job on any Hollywood movie set that I could.

Central Casting sent me to work an all-nighter on the Fox Studios lot, to be an Extra rocking out to White Zombie in the club scene for the movie "Airheads."

It was a thankless job; an uncredited Extra. I watched the scene again recently and can't find myself anywhere on camera, not lurking in the dark corners of any shot, nothing.

I was there, though, paired with a gorgeous blond girl. I don't remember her name, so for remainder of this story she will simply be referred to as, "Gorgeous Blond Girl."

"You two are boyfriend and girlfriend," the assistant director told us. "When we say 'action,' you just start rocking out."

Simple enough.

Life on a film set has a lot of down-time, though. So, Gorgeous Blond Girl and I had a full evening to hang out together. We were comfortable enough with each other, but she dropped The Big Warning early in the conversation.

"The Big Warning" is a girl very casually - almost TOO casually - dropping the phrase, "Oh, my boyfriend - "

It doesn't matter what the rest of the sentence is. She just let you know she's off limits. Some guys take it as a challenge. I accepted it without a second thought.

The club scene in "Airheads" has Chris Farley as a cop, entering the club, getting knocked around a mosh pit by some tough guys, and then finding the character he's looking for at the bar.

We had to shoot different parts of it over and over all night, trying to get White Zombie's performance right, trying to get Chris Farley's mosh pit moment right, etc.

We were still early in the process, during a quiet moment between shots, when Chris Farley was randomly standing just a few feet from myself and Gorgeous Blond Girl.

"What's your name?" he asked her.

She answered.

He followed up with a few casual remarks and a joke or two. She responded flatly, and soon everyone had to return to their marks for another take.

"That was awkward," she whispered to me as Farley walked away.

"And the evening's still young," I said.

"Oh, god, no," she sighed.

Then someone yelled 'Action.' White Zombie rocked their song again. Gorgeous Blond Girl and I rocked out.

Cut!

"Tell me he's not coming over here," she said to me when things quieted down again.

"He's coming over here," I said.

"God! No," she whispered.

Chris Farley turned on the charm this time. He was a celebrity, and he knew he could get what he wanted - most of the time.

She chatted politely with him, but stayed just cold enough to avoid encouraging him.

We rocked out to White Zombie some more, and then she proposed an idea to me.

"Hey," she said, hesitantly at first, "do you think, um, maybe we could actually pretend to be boyfriend and girlfriend, maybe just enough to get him to stop?"

"Sure," I said, smiling. "I'm game."

The next time things got quiet, and we were told to relax, I sat in a chair. She sat on my lap, dropped an arm over my shoulders, and when Farley started walking toward us she leaned close to my ear and teasingly whispered something to me, making it look like we were sharing a very private moment.

It worked.

Chris Farley was smooth.

He stopped in front of a brand new gorgeous girl, making it look as if he had been eyeing her the whole time.

The new girl seemed more open to his celebrity advances.

Gorgeous Blond Girl was off the hook.

As actors we were a little deeper into character the rest of the evening. We were boyfriend and girlfriend until about four in the morning. Then we went our separate ways, never to see each other again.

A few years later Chris Farley was dead, from a lethal combination of drugs.

He left a legacy of brilliant comedy and mediocre movies.

Perspective?

Hell, I don't know.

Maybe someday I'll get a chance to ask his old buddy, David Spade.

26

Cobain/Van Gogh

(Written in April, 2014, the 20th anniversary of Kurt Cobain's death)

This month marks the 20th anniversary of Kurt Cobain's death, and while countless articles are rehashing the same old themes, I want to float an idea out into the world that has been on my mind for...well, for 20 years.

First, I should say on a personal note that while I can count one or two Seattle musicians from the grunge era as friends, I never actually met Kurt Cobain. I blew off a friend's show once, not knowing until later that it would have been my one chance to hang out backstage with Kurt.

I do feel some personal connection to his loss, through friends who knew him and talked about their own personal memories after he died.

This isn't about my personal feelings, though.

I want to put Kurt Cobain into some sort of historical perspective.

To me, Kurt Cobain was the late 20th Century's musical Vincent Van Gogh.

Both were brilliant, troubled artists. Both probably suffered from some form of diagnosable mental illness.

Both were part of artistic 'movements' that caused them to be in conflict with the 'establishment.'

Both even suffered from severe PHYSICAL problems that contributed to their downward spirals (Van Gogh's ringing ear, Cobain's aching stomach).

Van Gogh came up as a painter among France's 'impressionist' movement in the late 1800's.

More than 100 years later the impressionists (Monet, Manet, Renoir) seem tame, but at the time they were revolutionary. They purposely broke all the establishment rules of painting. You could see their brush strokes. They painted sunlight informally as it really looked during different times of the day. They rejected posed mannerisms for candid movement.

They were the art world's punks.

Among this group, Van Gogh was an extremely volatile, insanely talented presence.

The comparison between the rebellious Impressionist movement and the 80's punk rock movement - which evolved into the 90's grunge era - doesn't seem too far of a stretch to me.

It's not a perfect comparison, but it's a reasonable one.

Cobain also had a volatile, but insanely talented presence in his movement.

Both Van Gogh and Cobain expressed their anguish, their volatility, their compassion, and their internal conflicts honestly and daringly.

Both suffered downward spirals that resulted in tragedy.

Both remain losses that are hard to explain.

Everyone who writes about Cobain tries to find adequate words to make sense of his too-short life.

I feel those words are not too difficult to find. They are simply:

Kurt Cobain, one hundred years later, was music's Vincent Van Gogh.

27

Soccer, Noses, and Doctor's Advice

(Written during the 2014 World Cup, hosted by Brazil)

The World Cup began a couple days ago. Every four years life stops for a month as soccer dominates everything.

This means that the only thing I'm interested in writing about is soccer.

First, as a side note, I am comfortable referring to the sport as either soccer or football. The word 'soccer' originally came from England. The word 'football' comes from everywhere in the world. I am also comfortable with the word 'calcio,' which is what the Italians have called the game, both in its current form, and in previous forms going back about 500 years.

So…what am I going to write about soccer? I'm not going to write about the sport itself.

I am going to write about my nose.

I broke my nose in a soccer practice, one day when I was seventeen years old.

I was trying to out-jump my teammate Martin to head the ball as it came down out of the air. Being a practice, we had split up the team and Martin was playing against me.

Things happen in split seconds on the soccer field. Martin won the header. I snapped my head toward the ball a millisecond too late. My attempt to head the ball resulted in a collision between my nose and Martin's head.

Blood was everywhere.

My chin, my shirt, the ground below me, was all blood red.

Our coach suspended practice, put me in his car, and drove me to the hospital. The Doctor poked around inside my nose with some tools, straightened it out to about 3/4 or 7/8 of its normal straightness, and then gave me a choice.

He said I needed a more thorough procedure to fully repair my nose. I could have it done right away, and be medically banned from playing for several weeks until it was 100% healed. Or I could live with the slightly crooked nose and be cleared to play again in a week.

I took the second choice. I didn't want to miss games.

The Doctor made me promise that I would have the procedure done sometime in the next few years.

I never had it done.

Years later, my nose is still slightly crooked. It isn't too bad. In some pictures you can hardly tell. Up close it is noticeable, though.

Whenever I notice it, looking in a mirror, it just reminds me that I once chose to keep the crooked nose, because I didn't want to miss soccer games.

Now it is a lifelong reminder, and maybe, just maybe a bit of a badge of honor.

28

Rising Waters

I don't want to think about how much it was. I certainly don't want to SAY how much it was. But I just dropped off a check covering the deposit on a new apartment I will move into on the 1st of next month.

It's in Venice, California, a block and a half from Venice beach. The end of the continent.

I've lived in Venice before. Twenty years ago I was in the neighborhood for two years. I'm not really a beach person, but I prefer the beach to the freeway.

A friend asked me, jokingly, "Do they speak Italian in Venice in California?" I said, "No, they speak Dude."

I remember heading out to the beach one December - I don't remember what year it was - when the cold wind was whipping in off the water so intensely, I could barely stand up straight. I was the only person at the beach that day. "This is the right time to come to the beach," I thought to myself, "when it reminds you that it's part of nature."

As I walked down the street in front of my new apartment building, I looked out at the serene-looking water, wondering how many years would pass before ocean levels rise enough to turn my street into the real Venice. Grab a boat and paddle. Welcome to Venice.

I recently watched a documentary about a sea port Caesar Augustus built two thousand years ago. Historians investigating the site now have to deal with the reality that water levels are three feet higher today than they were in Augustus' day.

Three feet in two thousand years.

How many years for the next three feet?

I'll write something about it if I need a water rescue from my apartment.

I don't really look forward to moving day. Lots of carrying and loading and pulling things up a flight of stairs. I'm glad to be back in the neighborhood, though. I recognize a guy on the Venice boardwalk who has been playing a guitar while roller blading, for twenty years now. He hasn't changed too much in twenty years. Maybe the lines in his face are a little deeper. But he doesn't care. He skates around the boardwalk, wailing away on his guitar. Not a bad life if you ask me.

The apartment itself is tiny, as apartments go. Apartment hunting in L.A. is pretty brutal. New York is probably ten times worse, but the process of trying to find a place - and beat out all the other applicants - has left me feeling a little punchy. Walking into places in my price range and wondering how the hell I get my stuff in here; being beaten out for places that were perfect; finding decent places I can afford, in neighborhoods that are less than ideal (Watts and Compton have great deals, really).

So, in the end, I plant my roots in Venice - not the Italian Venice, the Dude Venice. And I sit and wait for the waters to rise.

29
Customer Service

Call #1:

    Hello, my name is Tricia. Thank you for calling Time Warner Cable. I'll be doing whatever I can to make your day miserable. Can I have your full name and account number?

    Um, my name is Peter Wick, and the account number is _____.

    Okay, great. I have your account up here. What can I do for you today?

    I'll be moving on the 1st of the month. So I need my TV service moved to the new address at that time. I also will need your internet service added at the new address as well.

    Okay, I see you have our basic cable TV service. We have a bundle that I think would be perfect for you, Cable, phone and internet for a package price of $_____.

    No, I don't want phone service. I have a cell phone. I just want my cable moved and internet added.

    I understand, but this is the most inexpensive package we have.

    But it costs more than just adding internet to my current service, and I don't want the phone.

    Actually, just adding internet to your existing service will cost, $_____. So as you can see it is cheaper to get the bundle with the phone.

    How can that be? Why is it cheaper to get three things, including one I don't want, than to just get the two things I want?

    That's just how we work at Time Warner.

    I don't want the phone.

    Of course you don't. No one does. We force you to get it by talking around in circles like this.

Call #2:

    Time Warner Cable. Tricia speaking. How can I help you?

    Hi, I spoke with you yesterday. I decided to go ahead and sign up for your bundle, even though I don't actually want the phone.

    I see. Actually we currently have you signed up for a different package, including having one of our representatives call you each day to yell obscenities at you, for the new price of $_____. We have you scheduled for an installation appointment Tuesday between 8 am and sometime next year.

Call #3:

Hi, I was supposedly scheduled for an installation appointment today, but haven't seen any sign of the technician. Any word on when this guy is going to show up?

Oh, actually, that appointment was cancelled.

Cancelled?!

Yes.

By who?

By someone in our Trivial Annoyance Department. It seems the order was written up wrong, and the technician felt he needed more time than what was scheduled.

Was anyone going to bother telling me it was canceled? I dropped some work today, so I could sit around all day waiting for this guy.

No.

Hm?

No, no one was going to call you to tell you the appointment was cancelled.

Call #4

Time Warner Cable, Tricia speaking. How can I help you?

Hi, Peter Wick again.

Hi Mister Wick. Are you calling to sign up for our premium package? It includes HBO and Showtime, as well as several very expensive but murky and unspecified services that will show up on your bill as 'various fees.'

Uh, no, no I didn't call up for that reason.

Oh, I'm sorry to hear that. What can I do for you?

Well, I have in my hand a paper bill for my old address, with the old services, charging me for next month.

Mm hm, and what seems to be the problem?

Well, I mean, I cancelled service at the old address. I have different services, at a different price at a new address. So, I'm wondering why you're still expecting me to pay for services where I no longer live.

Oh, because we were hoping you wouldn't notice, and just pay without questioning.

I see. Well....I'm questioning.

Rats! There goes part of my commission.

And, one other thing...

Yes?

I went without service for 11 days at the beginning of the month. Any chance I can be credited for the days I had no service?

Hm, let's see, would you be willing to pay an additional thirty-five dollars for that service?

No, no, see, what I'm asking is if you can credit me back a little money because I received no service for eleven days.

I understand, Mr. Wick. I'm just asking you if you are willing to pay for that?

Pay for that! NO, see a credit means you give me some money back, or you deduct it from my next bill.

Exactly, Mr. Wick, and we are willing to credit you Fifteen dollars back, if —

If? If what?

If you are willing to pay thirty-five dollars for the service fee.

The service fee?

To process the credit.

You know what, never mind. I'm thinking seriously about just going out to see live entertainment every night.

What are you saying, Mr. Wick?

I'm thinking seriously about just cutting the cord and going without cable.

Hmm, that would be very expensive.

Expensive!? No, I would have to pay nothing. I would have no cable.

We charge a base price of two hundred dollars a month for that service.

What service?

Well, Mr. Wick, you must certainly understand that if it costs a certain amount for us to run cable entertainment and internet, not to mention the phone that you famously do not want, into your apartment, just imagine how much it costs for us to go away.

What do you mean?

Two hundred dollars a month to get us out of your life, Mr. Wick. That's our most prized service. Many people are willing to pay quite a lot for us to leave them alone. Are you willing to go down this road?

You know what, never mind. Just shut up and stop being so silly.
I would, but...
But what?
I would have to charge you for that service.

30
The Cosby Concept

As a very young child at the beginning of the 1970's, I remember life being more or less one big laugh after another.

This is selective memory, of course. There was a lot of heavy non-laughter in my young life, as there is for everyone. My most vivid memories, though, seem to highlight the crazy, the wild, the humorous, and the amusing.

I was one of five kids, in a household out of control. My parents seemed at a loss. It wasn't just us three brothers. My two sisters contributed to the craziness as well. We lived in a medium-sized house on Lake Sammamish, about 20 miles from Seattle. When my sister Keren and I decided to find out what lake water felt like during freezing December temperatures, my Mom wisely stayed quiet. Keren and I changed into swim suits, opened the front door and ran down to the beach. We knew we were doing something ridiculous. That was the whole point of it. Be ridiculous.

We also knew, vaguely, that what we were doing was stupid, but we wanted to learn just HOW stupid it was first hand. We didn't want to take some grown-up's word for it. We had to go down to the freezing water and get in. So we did. It was COLD. It was FREAKIN' COLD! We ran in as far as we could before instantly screaming and running back up to the house. My mom just seemed amused. She probably thought we had learned our lesson. We had, but the lesson had two parts to it; first, yes, we learned never to run into a lake in the middle of December. (I mean, it was freakin' COLD!) Second, though, we learned that on some deeper level, it was damn good fun to flaunt our ridiculousness for all the world to see. Who else in either my school class, or my sister's, could brag that they had gone swimming in the freezing lake in the middle of December? It was a cocky brag because we both knew it was untouchable in its credibility.

Into this laughter-filled childhood world, came a performer of unusual and brilliant charm. I don't remember which album entered the house first. There were several; "Bill Cosby is a Very Funny Fellow...," "I Started Out as a Child," "Revenge," "Why is there Air?" I don't even remember the comedy bits anymore. My memory is like an impressionist painting of moments. Cosby's voice playing characters, telling stories from childhood, making me laugh with his creative, magical stories. We couldn't see the performance. We could only listen to Cosby's voice, but that was enough. It was eye-opening.

When "Fat Albert" came along it was a natural must-see for a while.

Life as a child is always in flux, though. Each year brings a whole world of new interests and new fascinations. I don't remember losing interest in "Fat Albert." I just know that it was on my radar for a while, and then it wasn't anymore.

I became a teenager and wanted edgier fare. My comedy needed some bite to it. Before "Bill Cosby: Himself," came along in the early 80's, I had become a loyal fan of ground-breaking comics like George Carlin and Richard Pryor. I didn't expect much from "Himself." I remember watching it with my girlfriend, though, who did not have the same Cosby background that I had. To her, Cosby was just some guy. To me he was THAT guy, the guy from my childhood, the kids guy, the brilliantly funny kids guy.

"Bill Cosby: Himself" was a masterpiece. Unlikely as it seemed, my girlfriend and I were won over. We watched many episodes of "The Cosby Show" together, losing interest maybe three seasons in, as life provided - again - edgier fair.

Cosby was "Cosby." He wasn't just a performer, or a celebrity. He was a concept. Cosby epitomized 'safe' middle class classiness. Uncontroversial, rooted to daily life, and still creative and brilliant.

Life went on.

A few years ago, I happened to catch Cosby, now in his 70's, on Jimmy Fallon (The Late Show, before Fallon took over the Tonight Show). It was a fascinating performance. Cosby for some reason ended up sitting on the floor, doing stand-up from a previously un-tried position. Then as his age began to take over, he began to improvise (it had to be improvised) about how, at this age, you should never get down on the floor...you see, because you might never be able to get back up. Fallon got down on the floor next to him and they conducted the most unusual, hilarious interview I'd seen on late night television.

I felt comforted afterwards. Maybe Cosby was not the number one influence in my life, but he was there. He was deep in my psyche, going back to childhood, and it felt comforting to know that he was still COSBY in old age.

When the recent avalanche of sexual allegations poured down on him, from more than a dozen women, allegations of disturbing, secretive, predatory behavior, dating all the way back to the 1970's, I needed some time to process what was happening.

As a society we sometimes respond to celebrity scandals with ever-shifting double standards. Sometimes we are ready to drop a favorite celebrity instantly. Other times we forgive or we wait patiently, allowing for the presence of uncertainty to weigh on our judgment.

Michael Jackson's child abuse allegations are a case in point. I had little patience for Michael Jackson after that episode, yet many fans held tightly to the lack of a legal conviction, and gave him continuing support, respect and love until his untimely death.

I lost faith in Bill Cosby fairly quickly, and surprisingly (surprisingly for me, anyway) easily. It was a sad moment. Cosby meant something to me. Yet, I had little trouble wrapping my head around the concept of that near-perfect middle-American ethos, hiding dark, disturbing, criminal secrets. It made sense in that it didn't seem at first to make any sense at all.

Perhaps the 'Cosby thing,' that too perfect image, was so powerful that behind the scenes, deep in his own heart, he believed he had carte-blanche in the world.

As I write this, Cosby has not been proven guilty of anything....yet. In a criminal sense, he is innocent until proven guilty. One wants to be fair and give him the benefit of the doubt until something as conclusive as a court judgment either convicts or acquits him.

Even without that, though, the weight of the allegations, the number of women, the manner in which they came forward, collectively and individually, make it impossible to maintain faith in either Cosby as a person, or 'the Cosby concept' as a cultural ethos.

Chris Rock said "We lost Cosby this year," even though Cosby is still alive.

Chris Rock is right. We lost Cosby. The Cosby influence in our culture - and it was huge - is dead. Or it is dying. It is terminally ill.

It is a sad passing, because, as Cosby titled one of his early albums, I started out as a child.

31

The Once and Future Sonics

(Written during the NBA playoffs of 2015)

I am a coffee drinker.

And a basketball fan.

And from Seattle.

These three facts combine, this time of year, to cause a churning inner turmoil.

Why?

If you have to ask, you obviously are unaware of the evil that lurks beneath the surface of the beautiful game of NBA basketball.

It has been seven years since Howard Schultz, owner and CEO of Starbucks Coffee (not evil), sold his then-ownership (evil) of the legendary basketball team Seattle Supersonics to Oklahoma's Clay Bennet (very evil). The two men lied to the Seattle media about their intentions ("not") to move the team, all the while encouraged by then-NBA commissioner David Stern (most evil of all) to pack up the beloved team and ship them down to Oklahoma City to take on the new team name "Thunder."

During the years since, Seattle has had to go to court to make Oklahoma City return the 1979 Championship trophy. They have had to get another court injunction to keep the name "Sonics" in Seattle. And perhaps most galling of all, the greatest Sonic of all time, legendary point guard Gary Payton has had to turn down invitations from the evil impostors (OKC) to retire his jersey in a strange city where he never played. Payton (not evil...in fact a shining beacon of GOOD in this dark world) is to be commended for his loyalty to Seattle.

Perhaps a little perspective and background is in order.

The Chicago Bulls of the 1990's were evil. Yes, I am talking about Michael Jordan's 6-time winning Bulls.

By the way, the greatest player of all time has the initials MJ, but he is Magic Johnson, not Michael Jordan.

Anyway, Gary Payton, Shawn Kemp, Detlef Shrempf, Nate Macmillan, and many other shining beacons of GOOD in the world, coached by the brilliant George Karl, faced the Chicago Bulls in the 1996 NBA finals. People laughed. Most of the world was certain the Bulls would run all over the Sonics. What you don't know is the evil coach Phil Jackson performed several evil, satanic rituals, even sacrificing a wild marmot to the Prince Of Darkness, securing a devastating back injury to Nate Macmillan, thus ensuring that the evil Bulls would win a series that the Sonics WOULD have won, had there not been so much Satanic intervention.

I could go on. I could give you proof (secret photos of Phil Jackson performing ritual sacrifices to Satan, etc.) but I am a forward-looking person.

I have come to terms with my disappointment in Howard Schultz. For a while after the sale I boycotted Schultz' other business, Starbucks, but being addicted to coffee, I broke down, and finally decided I'll buy coffee from the guy. I just won't ever let him own a basketball team again.

I live in L.A. now, where I have been joking with Lakers fans for a few years, "What would you do if I declared myself a Clippers fan?" Lakers fans laughed.

Secretly, I already was a Clippers fan. Once Chris Paul joined the team, I recognized a Gary-Payton-like talent. When Doc Rivers became coach, I was hooked. When that old racist moron was forced to sell the team to Steve Ballmer (who, being a former Microsoft CEO, has that much needed Seattle connection) I made the commitment. The Clippers are winning and the Lakers are on vacation.

The one thing missing from my basketball life?

The Sonics.

They will rise again. I have faith.

After writing this, I suppose I'll have to answer a lot of questions about calling certain people evil. I will just state once again, these are facts. I can't reveal my sources, but it is well known that Michael Jordan, Phil Jackson, David Stern, Clay Bennett, Howard Schultz, and whoever else I happen to dislike in the game of basketball, comprise a secret society where sacrifices are made, souls are bought and sold, and the forces of darkness are used to compromise all that is good and pure in basketball.

At least Gary Payton won his championship in Miami with Shaq and Dwayne Wade in 2006.

What's that you ask? Didn't Shaq play for the evil Phil Jackson during a 3-peat by the Lakers? Sure, but, you know, anyone who liked Gary Payton enough to want him as a teammate....can't be ALL evil, can he?

Hm? What's that? Hey, stop asking questions, and just accept what I say.

32

Abducted

The 15-minute walk up Rose Avenue from my apartment to the nearest over-priced grocery store (that would of course be Whole Foods) is a colorful and interesting walk. You are sure to be surprised by something along the way. If it's not the giant ballerina-with-a-clown-head on the wall of the CVS Pharmacy, maybe it will be the neighborhood medical pot store, or the stenciled sidewalk art - a sinister looking silhouette of a man pointing up at you with the words, "You love the man," stenciled next to him.

You might be surprised by the sheer number of society's outcasts. There's a unique breed of homelessness in Venice, but that's another issue, to be dealt with at another time.

Taped or stapled to the streetlight poles and power poles are the usual posters; a band playing somewhere, a missing cat, a missing dog, a missing person...

It was along these lines that one particular flier taped to a pole caught my attention recently. At the top in bold letters was the word "Abducted!" Below the word was a picture of a bearded 20-something-looking guy.

I stepped closer to read the rest of the poster. It stated that this guy was abducted by aliens on a particular day, at a particular time, in Topanga Canyon. Then it said, "If you have any means of alien contact, please call us," and then it listed the phone number.... and that was it.

The poster raised a lot of questions for me, more questions than it could ever hope to answer.

Did the people making the poster actually SEE their friend get abducted by aliens? Even if you are able to contact these aliens, what will you say to them? Can you negotiate an abductee's release from alien capture? If you can negotiate an abductee's release, how do you negotiate? Do you offer a trade? Some other human to experiment on in exchange for the return of your friend? If you can negotiate a trade, who do you trade for? Do you look for a volunteer, or do you trade away someone against their will?

I nominate Kim Kardashian.

I plan to contact the President in the next few days and arrange a trade negotiation, in which we give the aliens Kim K in exchange for the return of whatever-the-hell-his-name-is - let's call him "Topanga Dude."

It's a beautiful trade, the more I think about it. I want to be there when the alien ship comes down through the Canyon trees and touches down gently on the roadway. Then the hatch slides gracefully open. Topanga Dude steps awkwardly out of the space craft, shielding his eyes from the bright light of the many car headlights. Kim K is then presented to the aliens. She whimpers a little as the government agent pulls her by the arm toward the craft. Several cars away Kanye shrugs and smiles as she is ushered into the craft and the hatch closes.

Moments later the craft - and Kim - are gone, never again to return to Earth.

One of Topanga Dude's friends asks him if he's okay.

"Sure, I guess," he says.

"What did they do to you?" a friend asks.

"Mostly they just made me scrub their toilets," he says. "Oh, and they did experiments on my brain."

"Cool," the friend says.

Then we all get in our cars and go home, never to hear about Kim Kardashian ever again....

...And there was peace on Earth from that day on....

33

Social Media has Saved the World

They say the first step toward healing is admitting the truth. Well, world, let's admit it, we're a pretty dumb lot.

This isn't a new phenomenon. Dumbness has run rampant since the first Homo Erectus decided to stand upright, and his dad yelled at him to quit showing off. "Walk bent over, like a normal early ape creature, yu damn kid!"

In the ancient world prior to the advent of social media - you know, the 1990's - dumbness was alive and well. (Two words....boy bands). Now we have Facebook, Twitter, Instagram, Snapchat, Google Plus....sorry, my mistake, we don't actually have Google Plus.

The great thing about this era of social media, is that we are living out Mark Zuckerberg's dream of a 'more connected world.' Being connected will save us....from....I don't know what. I was just reading about the person who was so excited about getting a new American Express credit card, that they posted a photo of the card in their Facebook status, not realizing the dangers of posting your new credit card number on the internet for everyone to see....and copy.

Then there was the guy who complained that his Science Teacher was so dumb, he thought the sun was a star. When someone replied, "That's because it is," he argued forcefully that, "A sun's a sun. A star's a star. there's a difference. Duh."

Reading posts like these give some insight into our society. Don't get me wrong. We are not dumber than we used to be. Our dumbness is just more exposed for all to see.

For example, I was stunned to learn something about disgraced bicycle champion Lance Armstrong that I had not previously known. One thoughtful person posted, "We should all get off Lance Armstrong's back. Sure he did drugs, but he was still the first person to land on the moon." Fascinating! I did not know that!

The examples are too many and too mind boggling to list. ("Canadians are so stupid they think 'Titanic' was a real event, not just a movie").

Mark Zuckerberg wants to save the third world, by floating wifi balloons around the world, so everyone can have access to Facebook.

Well, if Mark Zuckerberg believes it, it must be true, right?

I don't remember which of these are Facebook and which are Twitter (Twitter, by the way, is far superior, because I love Twitter). It doesn't really matter. What matters is that someone took the time to ask publicly whether "The Hunger Games" is a true story....failing to account for the fact that it is set in the FUTURE.

There's the person who posted, in full wonderment, "Can you believe this Earth is now 2015 years old? Amazing!"

"Why did they invent other languages? What, like one wasn't enough?" This person would be fascinated to learn that English is just about the LAST language to develop on the planet.

Or, the girl who asked why Chinese people don't have 'normal' names, like Kathy and Emily.

Or, they guy who was sure the world only has seven countries.

Or........

Forget it, we all get the point.

In closing I leave you with a modified age-old question to consider:

If a tree falls in the woods.....and no one is there to pose for a selfie in front of it.....did it actually fall? If no one posts it to Facebook, or at least Instagram, does it even matter? Or, if it's posted, but by someone with only 40 friends, and no one 'likes' it, did the tree even exist to begin with, or was it just too lame for existence?

34

Funny, Sexy, Nanobots

I was alarmed to read recently that scientists are planning to insert tiny nanobots into our brains in the not-too-distant future. Ray Kurzweil, who has researched artificial intelligence for years, and now works at Google, has predicted that in about 20 years we will be able to insert tiny robots – 'nanobots' – into our brains, making us, in his words, "funnier…sexier…and better at expressing loving sentiment."

I think it's interesting that scientists these days are so concerned about being funny and sexy. Scientists have always been the classic examples of nerdy geniuses who are anything BUT funny and sexy. I wonder if this is the scientists' ultimate revenge; years of being the victim of clever put-downs, the heart-ache of watching the dream-girl leave with the sexier stud, have led the scientific community to INVENT their way to being funny and sexy.

The way it works, if I understand Mr. Kurzweil's explanation, is that tiny robots from DNA strands will swim around in the capillaries of our brains, allowing us to connect to the cloud. This will give us increased 'logical intelligence' and 'emotional intelligence,' and apparently, funnier comebacks, and more devastatingly sexy personas.

I wonder if this is just wishful thinking on Mr. Kurzweil's part.

Connecting our brains to the cloud may certainly give us quicker access to knowledge ("The 1915 Treaty of London? Of course I know which countries were involved") but will it really give us a funnier comeback when someone insults us?

Sure, you'll have instant access to the entire database of other people's clever comebacks. There's the generic comeback listed on several websites; "Did you hear that? It's the sound of no one caring" Or maybe you want to go more Groucho Marx; "I never forget a face, but in your case I'll be glad to make an exception." Or maybe you want to tap into the more whimsical but biting style of Oscar Wilde; "Some people cause happiness wherever they go; others, whenever they go."

Despite all of this database access, though, I wonder if tiny nanobots will give us the creativity to come up with our own brilliant, original funny line.

As for sexiness, well, this is an even wilder dream on Kurzweil's part. At the risk of sounding sexist; the vast of majority of men have no clue what makes a man sexy. Do we really believe scientists can program robots for sexiness?

Hold on, something just occurred to me; Mr. Kurzweil doesn't plan to insert these nanobots into his own brain at all. He plans to put them in OTHER people's brains. Aha!

Mr. Kurzweil you have been found out! You plan to get your revenge on that girl who broke your heart, by inserting pre-programmed nanobots into her brain that will make her fall desperately in love with you.

Why do I see images of a crazy, laughing madman, surrounded by devices and bubbling beakers, screaming manically into the night, in a dark castle at the top of a lonely hill? On the outside of the dark castle, stenciled in crazy-looking uneven lettering, is the simple word, "Kurzweil."

35

Awards Season
(From January, 2016)

Awards season in L.A. is a funny period of time. We've had the Golden Globes and the People's Choice Awards already. Coming up are the Screen Actors Guild Awards, the Critics' Awards, the Directors and Producers Guild Awards, then my favorite, the Film Independent Spirit Awards, and of course the Oscars.

Everyone in L.A. both loves and hates this whole time of year.

I am qualified to vote in the Screen Actors Guild Awards and the Film Independent Spirit Awards.

For the record, it doesn't matter where you live as you read this, anyone reading this right now, could vote in the Spirit Awards. All you have to do is pay your $95 yearly membership fee to Film Independent, and presto, you get to watch free films.

There are so many screenings happening for free, there is not enough time in the day to attend them all. As I write this I could be arranging to screen a dozen films over the upcoming 3-day weekend, but in reality I will skip most of them.

I have no connection to the Oscars, but I've talked to several people who do, and they all seem to share a love/hate relationship with the whole process.

Maybe the reason is that in the end it only sort of matters, which means that it also sort of doesn't matter who wins, who loses, who is 'snubbed,' or who is a surprise winner.

20 years ago I worked for two days as an Extra and a Stand-in on 'Forrest Gump.' I had an insignificant 2-day job, and none of the important people on that film will ever remember my presence. I was hired to be one of the 'All-American' college football players that meets President John F. Kennedy, and when I arrived was also given the behind-the-scenes job of standing in Kennedy's place while the lighting crew set up the lights. I will go to my grave, though, proudly boasting that I worked on one Oscar winner. But I recently googled the other nominees from that year and discovered what I had forgotten. The far superior 'Shawshank Redemption' lost out to Gump, and that is all you need to know about the Oscars. Winning means nothing. Winning probably means you were the second or third best film of that year (in 1969 Stanley Kubrick famously lost the Directing award for 2001 to Carol Reed and the musical Oliver).

I try to take the job of voting seriously. I mean, it's important to me that Hollywood has some alternative way to gauge success besides the skewed value of box office numbers. But let's be honest, it is a very flawed system.

I'm not going to name any names, or review any particular film, but I went to a screening recently, my first time inside the posh offices of CAA – one of the top, maybe THE top Agency in the business – at the Ray Kurtzman theater (or is it Roy? Jay?). The film was, well, let's say I just wasn't buying into it. I thought it was 'okay,' but by no means a great film. I was so disappointed, because I like the guy who wrote the screenplay. I had high hopes for it. I left the screening frustrated at what passes for a 'great' film.

A few days later the Oscar nominations were announced, and there it was, smack in the middle of the list of nominees for best film of the year.

I twisted my head a little and laughed.

Oh well, whatever, it doesn't matter. The producers are happy, I guess.

It's still better to have awards than not.

I'm always surprised at how many people have not heard of the Spirit Awards. I've been watching them for years. They happen Saturday, the day before the Oscars, and they're more watchable because no one dresses up (I've always felt that I could never go to the Oscars, because I would be sure to vomit directly on someone's $20,000 gown).

So....watch the Spirit Awards. Then skip the Oscars. No, wait, Chris Rock is hosting. I guess I could handle watching some of the show to see him.

Just know that there's one film on that Best Film list that, if it wins, I'll be laughing at the absurdity of it all.

36

VOTE for the Absurd Ideas Party!

(Written early during the 2016 primary campaigns...before the entire election itself became a joke)

I keep trying to avoid politics, but we have entered the 2016 primary season, and politics dominates the conversation.

I have been giving it serious consideration, and would like to announce that I am throwing my hat into the political ring for the second time in my life.

The first time was in college, many years ago, and I ran for student council on a solemn promise that if elected I would immediately resign from office. The campaign was not my idea. It was my editor on the student paper who suggested I run. As reporters we had been writing about one student council member after another resigning from office. I can't remember why, some silly college version of controversy surrounding these council members.

On top of that, new elections were coming up, and only five candidates were running for six council positions. We were reporting on it, and laughing throughout the newspaper office about the dysfunctional state of our college's student government.

After agreeing to the preposterous candidacy, I had my picture taken and saw it run on the front page of the paper next to the headline, "Wick announces candidacy; if elected, promises to resign immediately."

It was strictly a write-in campaign. We weren't able to get my name onto the official ballot, but we figured that with only five candidates running, any write-ins for me, should actually get me elected, right? Then I would fulfill my promise to resign.

The elections came, and I was informed that I had received ten write-in votes. I won, right? With six positions open, and the five official candidates elected, I had received the next highest number of votes. I should be elected to the sixth council seat.

As it turns out, the college didn't buy into the joke. I was never allowed to be sworn in as a student council member. I was never allowed to honor the votes of my ten loyal supporters. I was never allowed to fulfill my promise to resign immediately after being sworn in.

I hope to do better this time.

I am inspired by England's "Monster Raving Looney Party." This is a real party that has been around for 50 years in England. Their official websites simply lists their motto as, "Vote for insanity." Sound advice, if you ask me.

So, I am declaring my candidacy for President, of the "Absurd Ideas Party."

Our motto? "You're voting for insanity anyway, just admit it and make it official."

A few of our key platform policies:

FOREIGN POLICY:

-Rather than a standing army, we propose that all foreign enemies be dealt a harsh, biting, cutting dose of extreme sarcasm. We believe sarcasm is what has been missing from the foreign policy debate up to now. Taliban, Iran, ISIS, North Korea, even some in Russia and China had better develop thick skin and fast, because we are going after your weakest defense; your sense of humor!

TAXES:

We do believe the wealthy should pay more, but they won't have to do anything on their own. We intend to access their bank accounts and steal their money. That will be our new tax policy; steal from the rich. As for Robin Hood's follow-up to that (giving to the poor) we're thinking about it. We haven't decided yet.

We at the Absurd Ideas Party will be releasing new policy statements on other issues of national and international irrelevance very soon. We are preparing a statement outlining our proposal to relocate all chinchillas to Lichtenstein. In the meantime, please remember that we can't get onto any official ballots. So, again, this is strictly a write-in campaign.

See you at the ballot box.

37

Fools

"The first thing you learn in life is you're a fool. The last thing you learn in life is you're the same fool."

A character named Leo Auffmann said that, in Ray Bradbury's book, "Dandelion Wine." Bradbury wrote the book in 1957. He had already made a name for himself as a Science Fiction writer with "The Martian Chronicles," and "Fahrenheit 451." Then he wrote this delightful book about a 12 year old boy discovering what it means to be alive.

When I read the line it resonated in a personal and humbling way. I have learned over the years that I am a fool. I have also learned over and over, that I am the same fool. It is impossible to have any small semblance of self-awareness and NOT learn this simple, humbling truth.

It doesn't have to be depressing. You can learn that you are a fool, and still have the confidence to proceed in life.

When I watch and listen to the fools running for President, I am struck by the thought that they, universally, have not learned this most basic lesson in life. They are fools. They don't know it. We should all be wary of each and every one of them.

This is not to say that they are all equally foolish. Obviously some are worse offenders than others. I am making it a personal policy not to name names, but the ones who proclaim loudly and without a hint of irony that they are the greatest thing to come along ever, these people in particular are people we should run from as far and as fast as we can run.

Who then, you might ask, should we approve of? In a Democracy, who should we vote for

I haven't figured out the answer to this question.

There are those who have a long-standing policy of voting AGAINST. They vote against whoever they dislike the most. They don't particularly LIKE those who they vote for, but they rationalize their vote by saying, "Better than so and so."

I'm not convinced. Anytime you vote, you are, by default, voting FOR someone. Voting for someone implies that you support them. You approve of that person being in a position of power.

I am no longer certain if I can ever approve of anyone who would run for political office. I cannot, in good conscience, approve of anyone who thinks they should be President. I am beginning to think that the desire to run for President automatically disqualifies you from the job.

Perhaps I am suffering from a loss of faith, but I no longer support politicians. As a group, they are people to be disdained and disapproved of.

They consist of 'the bad,' and 'the worse.'

They are fools, and they don't know it.

I think the rest of us are all too aware of it.

38

May 5th; A National Day of...Prayer/Reason/Drinking

I don't know how I missed it, but apparently May 5th has been, for several years now, a "National day of prayer." People around the country honor the day, both inside and outside of government, regardless of the fact that we as a country do not, in theory anyway, establish any particular religion as the "National" one.

In response, California state Representative Mike Honda (representing the Silicon Valley area), has introduced a new bill to declare the same day, May 5th, a "National day of reason." It isn't right, he believes, that everyone is required to honor a day of prayer, since we as a country do not require religious belief. His 'day of reason' balances the spirit of the day with a thoughtful, non-religious twist.

I think this is an interesting idea, balancing prayer with reason, but what really makes me stop in my tracks and twist my head sideways is that the two groups are fighting over a day that has already been well established as Cinco de Mayo, an International day of binge drinking.

I'm not suggesting that these three things are completely unrelated. Prayer and binge drinking can go together naturally - "Oh God, please let me stop puking!" - but it sets up a three-way battle, and I think everyone already knows the winner.

I did a little reading about the history of Cinco de Mayo. Many people think it is a celebration of Mexican Independence Day. It's not. That happens in September. Cinco de Mayo is a celebration of a Mexican victory over French forces in a single battle, and it is so insignificant historically, that the holiday is virtually ignored in Mexico itself.

This is where American drinkers come in. Americans barely need an excuse to binge drink. I've spent many St. Patrick's Days wondering how many drunk celebrators are neither Irish or catholic. On Cinco de Mayo, it's safe to bet that most of the loud, slurring, stumbling partiers, are not Mexican at all. They just like to celebrate. WHAT they celebrate is secondary.

This gets me thinking again about the same day being a day of prayer and a day of reason.

I support the idea of the day of reason but, unlike prayer, I'm afraid the binge drinking gets in the way. It would be almost impossible to celebrate Cinco de Mayo, get shit-faced drunk, and then try to be reasonable and thoughtful.

I want to see someone try, though. It might be fun to watch. The thoughts, comments, and 'reasonable' observations people make after a half-dozen shots of tequila are worth remembering; "Dude, you ever really look at your hand? I mean, really fucking LOOK at it?" "Mexicans are okay by me, man. I mean, they invented tequila, they CAN'T be as bad as Trump says." "Dude, check out that girl…no she's fighting with him, they're breaking up…Dude, I'm going to save her night, fuck the boyfriend, I'll help her dump him."

As for praying and drinking, I expect these two things happen together all the time. In addition to the prayer listed above, I want to offer a few other prayers that will be natural and appropriate on the "National Day of Prayer," that is also Cinco de Mayo:

1. Please God, get this drunk asshole off of me.
2. God, make him shut up before I stab him with this fork!
3. Oh, God, not another shot of tequila!
4. God dammit! Where did I park my fucking car?!

And the next morning's always popular…

5. Oh God, please make it not be 6 o'clock already! Fuck!

39

Report From Planet Earth

Report from Planet Earth

Prepared by: Zorbatron Mega; embedded galactic researcher.

(With a slight apology to Douglas Adams)

Greetings from the third planet in the Sol system. I hope everyone is doing well back home on the home Planet. I've been embedded here on this small planet for a 'year,' as they call each of their trips around their star. I have been collecting information that will help us decide whether we can destroy this planet, and run the Galactic Bypass through this solar system.

After a year of observation and study, I am happy to report that we can destroy Planet Earth without a moment of regret.

While it is true that the planet is inhabited by a species of walking bipeds, called "humans," I have come to the conclusion that, while they are undeniably "life," they do not reach the intergalactic standard that would label them "intelligent life."

Having said that, let me make one thing clear; humans THINK they are intelligent. They can talk and communicate among themselves (although the female of the species seems to be in unanimous agreement that the male of the species does not communicate well at all).

They use soft-tissue in their cerebral cortex, fueled by water, electricity, and something called caffeine, to formulate 'thoughts' (I use the word loosely), and these thoughts prompt them to speak. I have spent much of this last year trying to decide which is worse, what they refer to as thoughts, or their desire to speak their thoughts out loud.

As a species, they are builders. Humans have over-run the planet to such a degree, that they have had to build large cities, where people squeeze in close to each other, in tall buildings. They have some degree of technology, but rather than using their technology to advance their intelligence, they just use their many devices to watch cute cat videos. Of the more than seven billion of them that exist, a small handful are smart enough to warn the rest that they are destroying their own planet. Often, though, these few smart ones are criticized for their 'doom-saying.'

And yes, it is true, humans are already destroying their own planet without our help. This is a big reason why I feel comfortable saying we can finish the job for them, blow the planet up, and build the Galactic Bypass.

Because there are a small handful of humans who are less dumb than most, I suppose we should save a small sampling of the species. We could transport a few scientists, a couple teachers, a writer or two, a couple other artists, and what is known as a "Professional Athlete," to our home planet, in order to salvage the best of the species. The rest are of little value. They are all politicians, TV commentators, business people, religious leaders, and dictators of small countries. No big loss. I think it is more than enough to save about ten of these humans. With a fresh start on a new planet, they may even develop into a new and better version of themselves. With the proper help and guidance, they may even, someday, achieve some small degree of actual intelligence. Hey, don't laugh, anything is possible if you dream big.

So, let's get started. I have ten humans selected for transportation already. Once they are on their new journey, we can blow planet Earth to smithereens, and build the Galactic Bypass.

Wonderful new days are ahead.

I'm excited.

40
Drunk Brits

Those who know me, know that I never miss a major soccer tournament. Once every four years I rearrange my life in order to watch all, or nearly all, World Cup matches.

There is no World Cup this year, but two other tournaments - The Copa America Centenario, here in the U.S., and The Euro Championships in France - are keeping me entertained. The game on the field is entertaining enough, but every once in a while the game of soccer offers a second form of entertainment; marauding drunk British fans.

Before continuing, I should remind everyone that I come to my opinion of the British as someone who possesses some British blood myself. I also have a little bit of Scottish ancestry, though, and I'm pretty sure it's my Scottish side that forms most of my opinions of the British.

When I read about gangs of drunk loud-mouthed British fans clashing with riot Police in Marseille before England's opening match with Russia, I laughed, but it was that sad sort of laughter, a sort of 'here we go again' head-shaking laughter.

The next day, as Russia and England battled on the field to a frustrating 1-1 draw, fans from both countries began fighting each other in the stands.

A day after that England and Russia were warned to keep their fans under control or risk being kicked out of the tournament. France announced that it was considering banning the sale of alcohol anywhere within the vicinity of stadiums where England would be playing.

If you attend a Premier League game in England, you are not allowed to drink alcohol in your seat while watching the game.

I was thinking about all these things while watching the other tournament, The Copa America, last night, with Argentina battling Bolivia in my home town of Seattle. I had to settle for the television broadcast of the game, although I would have loved to be up in Seattle, at the stadium, watching Leo Messi in person, with one of those stadium over-priced beers in my hand.

The contrast is striking. As I watched the Argentina-Bolivia game it struck me that at no time during any of the previous Copa America games was there any incident of violence or "Hooliganism." In fact Copa America crowds - many of them from places as passionate about the game as anywhere in Europe (Brazil, Argentina, Mexico) were having a big happy party in the stadiums. When the camera passed one group of people holding, and sometimes spilling some of their over-priced stadium beer on each other, laughing it off the whole time, I wondered what made the two tournaments so different.

America certainly can't claim any high ground when it comes to violence. What makes our stadium crowds different?

Oh! Then I realized what it was...

Drunk Brits!

Yep, that's all the explanation we need.

Bolt down your chairs. Stop selling alcohol. Lock the doors.

The drunk Brits are coming.

I wish I were a little more Scottish than I am. I'm going to need some serious protection from the drunk Brits when they read this.

41
The Trump University Course Catalog

(A lot has been made of the fraudulent Real Estate University named after Mr. Trump. Few are aware, though, that for a short time it was intended to be a full academic institution.)

Trump University is dedicated to bringing awesomeness to anyone who doesn't want to be a loser, and then sending them out into the world to make the world less stupid!

ACADEMIC DEPARTMENTS:

Department of Winning So Good in Business:

Hi, I'm Donald Trump, and I'm such an amazing business man. I'm so incredible. I might be the most amazing business man who ever lived. You'll never be as great as me, but if you sign up for my business classes, you might at least get a chance to meet me and marvel at my charisma.

COURSES:

-The Art of The Swindle

In this course we will take a closer look at the mysterious workings of the swindle; how to swindle someone without them knowing it; swindling your closest friends and family; and of course how to get swindled by me personally, and LIKE IT.

-How to Make Money by Going Bankrupt

Many people mistakenly feel that bankruptcy is a bad thing. This course will explain how you can use bankruptcy to your advantage, and actually make money in the process, while leaving some other poor loser holding the bag.

Department of Psychology:

At Trump University's Department of Psychology, we basically point out how all this mumbo jumbo about mental health came from a bunch of weak cry babies who never learned to just suck it up

COURSES:

-The workings of the MIND….and why yours doesn't

In this course we examine Mr. Trump's mind, and discover why everyone should think the way he does, because, you know, he just tells it the way it is.

-Sucking it up 101

All this nonsense we've been hearing about 'feelings' comes from a lot of whiney liberal nerds. End of story.

Department of Journalism:

Just kidding. Journalism is for sleazy sleaze balls.

Department of Science:

At Trump U. we have searched the world and hired only those Science Professors who are sensible enough to realize that Planet Earth is going to be just fine. There is no global warming. There's no drought. The damn Environmentalists are alarmist crybabies. Animals are smelly pests who need to be eaten as fast as possible. Whenever you hear some so-called "Scientist" claim that things are going bad, just punch him the nose and give him a wedgey. If that doesn't shut him up, steal his girlfriend, and push him back down to the ground. Just kidding, he doesn't have a girlfriend, and he never got up off the ground after the first time you knocked him down.

Welcome!

You will always be happy you spent your hard-earned, easily lost money at Trump University. You will come away with a Major in Greatness, and a minor in irresistible sexiness. The entire world will be jealous of you. Seriously. All those people who criticize you are just jealous whiners. Screw them

42

An Open Letter To Hackers

Dear Hackers;

Hi, it's great to finally sit down and have a conversation. I mean, we aren't really sitting in the same room together, and I don't know how many of you there are, but I'm still glad we finally have a chance to talk.

I don't know who all of you are. I know there is "Anonymous," and "Gucifer," and the Russians who hacked into the Democratic Party, and of course the North Koreans who hacked Sony a couple years ago. You may also include Wikileaks. I don't think Edward Snowden is part of this conversation. He's more of a whistle-blower who just happened to have access to classified material. There are many others who I haven't mentioned, I'm sure. We don't know who hacked the credit card system of Target and stole a lot of customers' credit card numbers. A friend of mine was in that group...the group of people who had their credit card numbers stolen, not the group who did it.

I first became aware of you guys several years ago, the first time some funny things happened to an old bank account of mine. That was seven or eight years ago now, and I don't even remember all the details anymore. That was also long enough ago that it probably makes you laugh to think back on those primitive hacking days.

Two years ago you hacked my Yahoo email account, forcing me to finally switch to Gmail. Friends of mine were getting emails saying they were from me, telling them that I was stuck in Greece and please send money. Most of my friends laughed when they got the email. "Peter's email got hacked," they all said uproariously. No one believed the email was real. Did you really think anyone would send money? I mean, come on. My friends are smarter than that. I did, though, start asking myself, "but what if I actually WERE stuck in Greece and emailed my friends for money?" It dawned on me that my friends would laugh it off the same way, and never send me any money.

Some of you, I know now, are embedded deep inside the Chase banking system. You know who you are, and Chase knows you are there, but they don't seem too concerned. When I closed my Chase account a few weeks ago, the banker asked me why I was closing the account. "You guys are hacked," I said. "They're inside your system." The banker was silent for a minute, and then said, "Well, we're pretty big, you know." I wasn't sure if this was her way of saying, Well, we're big, what do you expect? Maybe Chase is okay with your hacking presence, as long as you don't mess them up TOO much.

Some of you have hacked into the U.S. Government. You've leaked private emails from former Secretary of State Colin Powell. You have, I'm sure, hacked into very important and 'secure' computer systems world-wide, and are just waiting for the right moment to do something diabolical and shocking.

I received a fraudulent email recently claiming to be from the IRS (I'm smart enough to know that the IRS doesn't send emails). The email said I risked jail time if I didn't send money owed due to 'tax fraud.' Maybe that wasn't you guys. Maybe that's not really hacking. I suppose that's just old school scammers. So, if that was none of your doing, sorry. I don't mean to tarnish your image.

You see, hackers, you are winning, as far as I can tell. I realize this now.

Sometimes I'm supportive of this. I do believe in exposing government secrets to some degree.

What worries me is that those who are trying to stop you seem to be failing. The only good news I can find in any of this, is that maybe you are keeping the technology industry honest. Maybe you are preventing the powers that be from totally taking over our lives.

If I could ask just one small favor, though; do you think you could hack into ALL the big Hollywood studios, and rig their numbers so they think they have to STOP making only sequels and remakes? If you could twist their numbers so it suddenly looks like NEW ideas are the hot new thing, CREATIVE concepts are the sure bet....that would make me feel a lot better about all the future times you plan to hack my emails and bank accounts.

43

Happy National Cheese Curd Day

I'm not sure why I never thought of this before. A friend recently pointed out to me that there are many more national holidays than we actually celebrate.

For example, did you know that February 3rd is National Carrot Cake Day? July 30th is National Cheese Cake Day, and October 19th, a few days from now, will be National Seafood Bisque Day.

These holidays are all real. You can look them up on nationaldaycalendar.com. It turns out that anyone can submit an application to have a new holiday designated. Well, almost anyone. The website currently says that due to backlog they can only accept submissions from companies and organizations. So, sorry Freddy, you can't apply on your own to have September 5th become National Freddy Day.

I'm intrigued by this new world opening up to me. I want to know more. There are a lot of days that have multiple things designated to celebrate.

January 2nd, the day after New Year's Day, 2017, will be all of the following: National Buffet Day, National Cream Puff Day, National Personal Trainer Awareness Day (I will be sure to be aware of Personal Trainers on that day), National Science Fiction Day, and National Thank God It's Monday Day (because it will be the first Monday in January). Not to be outdone, Friday, January 13th, a couple weeks later will be: National Peach Melba Day, National Rubber Ducky Day, National Sticker Day, Stephen Foster Memorial Day, and National Blame Someone Else Day (because it is the first Friday the 13th of the year).

December 16th, interestingly, is Barbie and Barney Backlash Day.

I am beginning to work on a list of my own holidays that I want to apply for. Everyone knows I am a huge soccer fan, and I think we need a day each year – even years when there is no World Cup (ESPECIALLY years when there is no World Cup) designated as Celebrate The World Cup Day. The world is descending into a frightening state, these days, and I am convinced that the promise of upcoming World Cups might be the only thing keeping the world from blowing itself up. Maybe we should designate International Play Soccer Instead of Blowing Up The World Day.

I just now realized that the month of my birthday, April, is National Humor Month. April is also: International Guitar Month, National Soft Pretzel Month, National Straw Hat Month, and National Welding Month.

I've been hitting the stand-up comedy open mics again recently, after not being on stage for a long time. I have been in and out of open mics a lot during my lifetime. Even when a comic is working clubs and getting paid, he or she will still use open mics to try out new material or just to 'work out.' We need a stand-up comedy open mic celebration. Too often open mic-ers have to do their jokes in front of an audience that consists mostly of other comics, rather than real audience members. I want to submit National Stand-up Comedy Open Mic Awareness Day ("appreciate the half-written joke – applaud the idea – encourage a rewrite of the punch line").

The possibilities are endless. We might have an explosion of new holidays to celebrate.

Oh, just one last thought. November 8, 2016, will be National Don't Run For President If You're a Jackass Day.

44

The Ghost of Elections Past and Future

T'was the night before election day and everyone had gone to bed. Everyone, that is, except for Donald.

Donald had not slept in weeks. He sat restlessly on his gold-plated toilet wondering if he should use a laxative.

A face appeared in front of him. It was not a human face. It was a mysterious apparition that floated effortlessly in the middle of the room.

Donald blinked once, twice.

"Hello, Richard," the apparition said.

"R - Richard?" Donald repeated. "I'm Donald."

The apparition paused, looking slightly confused. It looked at a mysterious piece of paper that floated in mid-air.

"You have been running on 'law and order'?"

"Y - yes," Donald said.

"You have been claiming there is a hidden vote for you? A 'silent majority'?"

"....Yes."

"You have been keeping a list of enemies?"

"Well, sure," said Donald.

"You're Richard," the apparition said. "Richard Nixon."

"No!...No!"

"Sh - sh," the ghost calmly touched a hand to Donald's shoulder. "It's just a fact," the ghost said. "You are Richard Nixon."

"A f - a fact? What is that? I've heard of those, but never really got -"

"I know, I know," the ghost said with a sigh. "Facts are difficult to understand. I'll explain later."

"Who are you?"

"I am the Ghost of Elections Past."

"No! - No, it can't be. You aren't real. You're a figment of my imagination. It's because I haven't slept since 1993. You're a piece of undigested KFC. You can't be real!"

"I assure you, I am real, Richard."

"Donald! I'm Donald!"

"Calm down, Richard. It's okay."

"Why are you here?"

"I'm here to show you the past."

"No! Anything but th - "

But before Donald could finish his objection he and the ghost were whisked back to 1998.

Donald saw his younger self sitting in a room with a reporter.

"What's this?" Donald asked the ghost.

"It's you, in 1998, doing an interview for People Magazine."

Then the younger Donald spoke; "If I ran I would do it as a Republican. They're the dumbest voting block in the world. I could go out there and lie and they would eat it up."

"No! I never said that."

"Donald! The ghost looked sternly at him. "Donald, we just saw you say it."

"But - "

"Shut up. You said it. You can't keep pretending you didn't say things that you said."

Donald desperately tried to reach out to his younger self, but he was suddenly whisked back to the present.

He was again sitting on the gold-plated toilet.

"I really need a laxative," he said out loud to no one.

"I know how to shake your bowels loose," said a new mysterious voice.

Donald looked up, startled. A new apparition appeared in front of him.

"Hello, Richard," it said.

"I'm Donald."

"You want to know how we can shake those bowels loose, Richard?"

"How - who are you?"

"I am the Ghost of Elections Future."

"Oh, god, no. NO!"

"That's right, Richard, one glimpse of the future and your body will empty itself out like a popped balloon."

"It - it can't be that bad. I have such a good brain."

"Richard!"

"I'm Donald."

"You're Richard. Accept it. You will be the most erratic, emotionally immature, dishonest President since Richard Nixon, and you know how THAT ended, right?"

"No...NO, it can't be!"

"It's true, Richard. There's only one way it can end."

"I'll change. I'll do better. I promise."

"Too late, Richard. It's too late." And the ghost began to disappear.

"Wait. Come back. Aren't we going to visit the future?"

"Fuck that," the ghost said. "I've already seen it. Too depressing to see it again. I'm out."

"NO! Come back. I'll change. I'll - "

But the ghost was gone.

"I promise, I'll do better." Donald sank to his knees. "I'm sorry. I'm sorry."

Then suddenly he realized he needed to sit back on the gold-plated toilet asap.

Part Three
The Salvador Deli
A Story

"Hurry, Paul, you'll be late for work."

Paul stumbled groggily into the kitchen, bumping into the doorway, his eyes half closed.

"And where did you get these cigarettes?" Janey shouted, pulling a half-empty pack from his shirt pocket. Paul are you smoking again?" She looked intently at him. "Paul!"

"Huh? Mmgh, what's wrong with me these days? I just can't get going in the morning."

"Paul! Why do you have cigarettes?"

"Huh?" Paul looked genuinely confused. "What? I have no idea. You know I don't smoke."

"Then why do you have them?"

"Janey, I don't know. I don't know where they came from."

Janey gave Paul a sideways, questioning look, and tossed the cigarettes in the garbage. "Something strange is going on," she said.

Paul tried desperately to think, but his eyes closed again and he rested his head in his arms on the table.

"Here, I cooked you some eggs."

Paul sat up with a start.

"Paul, maybe you should get some time off. We haven't taken a vacation in a year and a half."

Paul groaned and tried rub some life into his eyes. "This is a bad time," he said. "If I want to be manager of the new deli they're opening in April, I gotta kill myself for 'em a little longer."

Sometimes he couldn't believe it. He had worked at the deli for, how long now? Thirteen years? Fifteen? Been an Assistant Manager for five, anyway.

"But you're so tired these days," Janey said, gently brushing his hair from his eyes. "And you'll only have to work harder if you become manager of the new one."

She reached out and opened the fridge, grabbing the carton of milk inside.

"No milk, please. Just coffee," he said. She stood up and pulled a coffee mug from the cupboard.

"Here, take these eggs away, too," he said. "I can't eat them."

She squinted at him, trying to make sense of his mood. She picked up the plate of eggs.

"No," he said, "it ain't working so much. I mean, I felt better last night than I do now. Really, I feel like I haven't slept a wink. I feel like I've been out all night. That's really how I feel."

Paul was an unusual case; the most brilliant musician the University of Minnesota had seen in years, wildly talented, erratically brilliant, but most notably, personally volatile. All this was in the past, though, a decade and a half in the past. All that he still had from those times was Janey. Sweet Janey. She had stuck with him when everyone else, all his other friends, had left. They moved to New York or L.A. or, in one case, London. He began working at the deli just to make ends meet while moonlighting nearly every night on the piano at a local bar.

For all his diverse talent and promise, his music of choice had always been jazz, and not big fancy jazz-band jazz, which he had received such glowing reviews for while at the University, but musty old piano-in-the-corner-of-the-bar jazz. So that is what he did for two years, without incident. Everyone thought he had found himself. They thought he finally had what he wanted.

A few of his friends quietly shook their heads when the topic of his blown chance with the Minnesota Symphony came up.

That was a story all its own; after playing brilliantly with the symphony for over a year, receiving wonderful reviews, he actually blew up during a concert. He threw the jacket of his tux at the conductor and stormed off stage.

So much for his 'career,' everyone thought.

There were murmurings among his friends that he had deliberately sabotaged his career, that he planned the blow up.

Paul didn't care what anyone thought. He had Janey and he had the piano in the corner of the bar.

For two years everything seemed fine. He worked at the deli, played piano, and made love to Janey.

Then, one night, Boom! He knocked the piano over, trashed the bar, and yelled until he lost his voice.

And that was that. He never played again.

No one, not even Janey, really understood what happened.

She didn't bring it up either. She knew Paul wouldn't talk about it even if she did.

All these years later the subject remained taboo.

Paul gulped down the coffee, sighed, and pushed himself up from the table.

Janey silently debated with herself. Should she say it?

"Maybe you should start playing piano again," she said. "Not seriously or anything, but maybe you can't sleep well because your dreams are troubled. I was watching a show yesterday where a psychiatrist said –"

"Janey!" he snapped. "We're not going to talk about that!"

"Sorry."

An awkward moment passed. She stood up, looked at the floor.

Paul cleared his throat and turned away.

"We – " Janey caught herself, then continued. "We haven't made love in over a month."

Paul paused for a moment, then grabbed his coat and walked abruptly to the door.

"I'll be home at seven," he snapped, and left quickly.

After he left Janey collapsed in a chair, exhausted. She didn't want to tell Paul, but she was awfully tired herself these days. Maybe they had a disease or something, she thought. Before even finishing the thought, she rested her head in arms on the table and fell asleep.

The Salvador Deli was more than just a deli. Set squarely in the heart of the Minneapolis business district, it was the preferred lunch spot for professionals from countless nearby businesses.

It had a huge seating area and offered a wide selection of deli sandwiches, salads, pizza, pasta, burgers, and alternative vegetarian and vegan faire. On the walls surrounding the seating area were prints of some of the greatest art works of the Impressionist, Expressionist, and Modern eras; works by Picasso, Chagall, Magritte, and of course Salvador Dali.

As Paul entered through the back door that morning, Charlie, the Manager, handed him a slip of paper. "Got a party of 20 coming in right when we open," he said.

"Right," said Paul, trying desperately to hide his fatigue.

"By the way," Charlie said, "Why did you put the garbage in the walk-in last night?"

"Huh?"

"The garbage. It's all in the walk-in. Normally we just throw it away. We seldom refrigerate it."

"Oh my god," Paul said quietly to himself. He played back the previous evening in his mind, he had switched the garbage with several batches of pizza dough. He could only hope Charlie was unaware that he had tossed perfectly good dough into the dumpster.

After Charlie left Paul shook his head vigorously a couple of times, slapped himself, and muttered a few words of motivation under his breath. "Come on, man," he said to himself, "it's all in your head. You're fine. Get it together!"

He finally convinced himself and moved confidently toward the swinging door that led out to the seating area. He pushed to door boldly, whacking Charlie, who was approaching from the other side, on the ear and wrist, knocking a stack of containers out of his hand and onto the floor. The door had cut a gash down the side of Charlie's face.

"Jeezus!" Charlie yelled, dabbing at the blood on his cheek. "You trying to kill me?"

Paul sunk to a squat, holding his head in his hands.

"Look," he said. "Maybe I shouldn'ta come in today. I haven't been feeling well. Is it alright if I go home?"

"By all means," said Charlie. "Geez! I want you as far away from me as you can get today."

"Thanks," said Paul, and yanked off his apron.

Outside, he zipped up his coat. He didn't want to go home, so he walked randomly down the street. His mind was racing. He tried to settle his mind down, but it wasn't cooperating. It was shifting erratically from a deafening internal din, to blank numbness, and then back again.

He looked distractedly into shop windows.

After a while he was overwhelmed by a nagging worry. He was feeling some of those old feelings; the anger, that old coiled up frustration that used to make him blow up. For several years now he had felt secure that he had been cured of these feelings, that he had outgrown them. That it was the music that did it to him, and divorcing himself from the music had finally cured him. So why, he worried, was he feeling some of those old emotional twinges flickering to life inside him?

He forced the thought out of his mind.

"Jack!"

He flinched. He looked up at the woman. He nearly did a double-take. She almost looked like Janey, but she was gorgeous, an absolute knock-out. She wore a sexy, revealing blouse, unbuttoned to show a little bra-less cleavage. She wore a sexy skirt, showing just enough thigh to make him awkwardly uncomfortable.

"Whatcha doin' up so early, or haven't you gone to bed yet?"

She slid her hand around Paul's buttocks and squeezed teasingly. Paul drew a sharp breath and audibly gasped.

"Maybe you need some help getting to sleep," she said coyly.

"I – I....I'm not Jack," Paul said. He stood awkwardly for a few seconds, then turned, walking away just as awkwardly.

He ended up at a coffee shop. He sat down with a muffin and a cup of coffee. He didn't touch either for twenty minutes. He sat, staring blankly. The he abruptly stood up and left.

"Paul, what are you doing home?"

Paul closed the kitchen door and pulled Janey into an embrace.

"Janey, listen, I'm sorry I snapped at you this morning. I don't – I don't know what's going on. I'm – I'm taking the day off. I just want to go lie down."

Janey kissed him and tightened the embrace. "Paul, Paul....Paulie, don't worry."

"Maybe you're right about needing a vacation," Paul said.

"Go lie down. We'll get through this. We always do."

"You're the best," he said, kissing her lightly.

He pulled out of the embrace and walked heavily toward the bedroom.

Paul slept straight through the day.

Janey, after several hours reading and watching TV, entered the bedroom and watched him sleep. She wanted to doze off herself, but she became engrossed in the restless display she was watching. Paul's sleep looked troubled. He tossed and turned. He moaned. He jerked his arms and legs. At one point he chuckled and said, "Mm, Chrissy." Janey cocked her eye at that and suddenly felt a bit more awake.

He smacked his lips a couple times and moved his fingers toward his mouth, as if smoking. Janey squinted when she saw this.

He seemed to settle down just slightly after this. His restless sleep calmed some.

Finally around eight o'clock Janey grabbed a bite from the kitchen and headed to bed herself. She kicked some clothes away from the bed on the floor. What a mess, she thought, clothes everywhere. She was too tired to even clean up these days.

She climbed into bed, kissed Paul lightly on the cheek, and closed her eyes.

Twenty minutes later, after Janey was asleep, Paul rose sharply up from the bed. He pulled on some pants and yanked a shirt from the closet. The shirt happened to have a cigarette packet in the pocket. He popped a cigarette in his mouth, lit it, pulled on some nearby shoes, and left with a look of mischief in his eye.

Moments later he walked into The Blue Lantern.

"Jack! You're early tonight."

Paul glanced at the four people circled around a table as he hung up his coat. "Are you complaining? What's wrong with being a little early? Or are you too much in shock to say anything intelligent?"

"Ha, freekin' Ha," said the back haired man at the table.

"Jack," said a red-haired woman, "we have an argument maybe you can settle."

"You people couldn't reach a conclusion if it jumped off the table and bit you."

"Play 'Takin' The A Train,'" said Suzy, the blond woman.

"For you, baby, I'll do any damn thing you want," Paul said.

"Hey!" said the man with the moustache. "I hope you don't mean that literally."

Paul smiled at the man. "Keep hopin', Randy. Just keep hopin'."

"I'm telling Chrissy," said Randy with a wry smile.

"Suzy and I can tell her ourselves, when we get together later for our threesome," Paul said.

Everyone at the table laughed.

"Ouch, that hurts," said Randy.

Paul looked at Suzy. She as smiling coyly. He turned at made his way to the piano.

There were a few other people scattered around the bar. A couple sat in the corner, sipping beer and talking quietly. A bearded man sat at the bar and brooded over his whiskey. Another man was hunched over a beer and a book.

Jack (yes, he was Jack now) played as much for the stranger as for his friends. Some were true strangers. Other he knew by sight, but had never spoken to. The man hunched over the book was there every night.

He tinkled the keys a little to warm up.

"Sam, when you gonna tune this thing?"

The man behind the bar yelled back, "You ask that every night, and every night it sounds perfect."

"Nah, it's close, but close and perfect ain't the same thing," Jack said.

"Shut up and play."

Jack lit into the keys with an energetic and heartfelt version of Duke Ellington's 'Takin' The A Train.'

Jack's head bobbed instinctively to the rhythm. At times he closed his eyes. He once said that he doesn't so much play jazz, as he becomes a vehicle for jazz. "It's a greater force than I am," he said. Jazz uses me. It goes through my body, through my hands, right through the piano. It's a connection with a greater force, a jazz force. The big jazz-man in the sky just takes over."

"You've gone off the deep end," Randy had responded that night.

"You're just now noticing?" Jack responded.

He took the A train as far as he could take it. When he finished he saw Chrissy standing at the end of the piano.

"Hi, Chrissy. God, you look gorgeous."

"You didn't think so this morning," she said.

"This morning! What are you talking about?"

"On the street. I know that was you. You ran off on me."

"I didn't see you this morning. It couldn't have been me."

"Come on. It was 9:30. You were acting real strange."

"That's because it wasn't me. Believe me, I would remember seeing you. Besides, I'm not up at 9:30. You know that. I'm like a vampire, only out at night. I'm the jazz vampire."

"Okay, okay," she finally agreed. "But there's an uptight pinhead out there who looks exactly like you."

Jack was still looking at Chrissy as he absent-mindedly began a slow song on the piano. "Besides," he said, as he massaged the piano keys, "I wouldn't treat you anything but right. You know that. I'd do anything for you, Chrissy."

She wiggled in next to him as he played. Jack glanced around the bar. The couple sitting in the corner were giving each other a kiss. Jack felt responsible for it. He smiled. He turned back to Chrissy. Still playing, never missing a note, he kissed her. They held the kiss for a moment, as they both felt a tingle go through them.

Jack pulled out of the kiss. "you felt it, didn't you? That tingle. It was the big jazz man in the sky."

"You're crazy," she laughed.

The evening wore on quietly and romantically. After an hour and a half Jack took a break from the piano. He and Chrissy sat down at the table with their four friends.

The conversation was light, often breaking into laughter. Jack and Chrissy smiled at each other often. They pretended to be interested in the conversation, but they were in their own world.

They could barely keep their hands off each other.

Eventually, their hands slid together under the table. Before long Jack took his hand from Chrissy's and rubbed it along the inside of her thigh, sliding it along her sleek black tights. She did not resist.

After a while Jack returned to the piano. He knew Sam expected a good three hours of playing from him. It wasn't something he was strict about, it was an unspoken understanding between them.

On nights like tonight, with Chrissy exuding sensuality, he found it difficult to concentrate. He tried, though. He did the best he could to focus on the music.

At two in the morning Jack and Chrissy were in the doorway of Paul and Janey's bedroom, kissing each other passionately. Clothes fell to the floor. Tongues intertwined. They breathed heavily together in rhythms heard only during moments of sexual abandon.

Later, Janey awoke spontaneously to the quiet peaceful serenity of the early morning. Paul lay next to her. She felt tired but peaceful, and a little more rested than she had felt a day earlier.

She looked at the clock. It was 6a.m. Paul would have to get up soon. Slowly, heavily, she swung her feet out of bed onto the floor. Her eyes fell on the clothes bunched up on the floor. There were those tights again, and that blouse and skirt. She must have been doing something in her sleep again, she thought. "Something must be wrong with me," she whispered to herself. "People don't throw old clothes out of their closets in their sleep."

She rose out of bed and headed for the kitchen. She slowly started a pot of coffee. She was surprised at just how good she started to feel. Not great, but certainly better than yesterday.

"I think I want to go back to school," Janey said, as she sat across from Paul.

Paul stabbed at a piece of egg, and shoved his fork in his mouth. "Really?"

"Yeah," she said. She sipped her coffee. "It bothers me that I never finished my degree. I mean, what am I doing with my life? Where's the time going?"

"You're planning to finish the same degree?"

"Well..." she looked at him. "Why not?"

"No, that's great. I just, I mean, a creative writing degree. There's not exactly a big industry clamoring for new hires."

I don't know." She stumbled over her thoughts. "Once I have the degree, then I could use it different ways, you know. Write, teach, maybe get into advertising or something."

Paul finished his eggs and smiled at her. "I think it's great," he said.

They shared a smile together. She felt relieved.

"I gotta run," he said, standing. "I'll try not to be too late tonight."

"Okay, see you tonight, honey."

They gave each other a kiss, and Paul left.

"I hope you're okay this morning," Charlie said as Paul walked in the back door. "We're going to be a madhouse today."

"Are we?"

"Look at this, two parties when we open, one of twenty, one of twenty-five."

"Jesus!" Paul said.

"On top of that, regular lunch is going to be hell. We were swamped yesterday with this convention in town, and today's Friday."

"I think I'm going to be sick," Paul said.

"Nope! Not today," Charlie snapped. "You can't be sick until tomorrow."

Paul knew what he had to do. He jumped right in. He wasn't happy about it, but at least he felt better than yesterday.

He started prepping pizza dough, salads, sandwich condiments. It was a busy morning, but Paul settled into a comfortable rhythm.

At eleven they opened the doors.

It was worse than they had prepared for; people everywhere, kids screaming, food flying, soda spilling.

After thirty minutes of it Paul noticed they were still a person short. "Where's Doug?" he yelled to Charlie.

"Just quit!"

"What!?"

"Just called and said screw all of us! He quit!"

"Did you call someone else in? We can't be short on a day like this."

"Everyone's scheduled for later tonight. No one's free."

Paul threw the olives onto the pizza he was making. It was getting uglier by the minute.

"Excuse me," a customer said, cutting in front of the line. "There are no clean tables. Do you think someone could come out and bus some tables?"

Paul threw the pepperoni down in frustration and grabbed a bus tub. He went out to the seating area.

"Hey, can we get our drinks?" Another customer yelled.

Paul looked up. "Where's Wendy?" He yelled to Charlie.

"Makin' pizza," Charlie yelled back. "You walked away."

Paul shook his head, left the bus tub on the table and went to the drink counter.

"What'll it be?" he snapped.

"Large Coke," the man said.

"Excuse me, are these tables going to get cleaned off sometime today?"

Paul heard this and pulled the cup away from the Coke nozzle. He looked down at the floor trying to keep himself together.

It was too late.

He threw the Coke cup at the floor, spraying several people with Coke. and stormed out to the seating area.

"Here," he said, "bus the fucking table yourself!" He turned the bus tub over and dumped what plates and cups were inside, down onto the table top. Two cups rolled of onto the floor and shattered in a spectacular crash.

"Hey!" the customer yelled. "What in the – "

"Just clean up the fucking place all by yourself," Paul yelled. Then he kicked a table over. "How's that? Happy now? Self serve! Get your own drink! Clean your own fucking tables!"

He picked up a half-eaten sandwich from the floor and moved toward the man. "Here's your fucking lunch. Looks like you didn't finish it. You have to fucking finish your lunch!"

Paul threw the sandwich at the man.

"Hey, Dude! Lighten up, man!" The man pushed Paul away.

Paul froze. "DO NOT......FUCKING TOUCH ME!"

Paul pushed the man back into a table with people at it, sending everyone scrambling and falling.

The place fell silent. All eyes were on Paul. He had a manic look in his eye. He stood up from the carnage of chairs, food, and frightened people.

He turned slowly from one person to another, breathing heavily, making eye contact with each person as he turned.

"Look!" he yelled, making everyone jump slightly. "I don't care about your fucking drinks! I don't give a shit, okay. You can all go cook your own fucking pizza! Fuck this place!"

He moved out from the middle of the mess, kicking chairs out of his way. He yanked off his apron and threw it at a customer.

He walked to the front door, passing Charlie, who shook his head in utter dismay.

Paul slammed the door as he left, and walked down the street in no particular direction.

After ten blocks of pounding the sidewalks, Paul finally began to slow his pace.

He began to breathe a little slower, and the reality slow began to sink in; he had just quit his job.

"Oh god," he said audibly on the sidewalk. "What did I do?"

He leaned against the wall of a building, sunk down to squat, and held his head in his hands.

After a few moments he took a deep breath, lifted his head, and slowly stood back up. He began walking again. His pace was slower than before. His head was spinning. He had to figure something out, but his head was a dizzy blur.

A few blocks later he found himself looking at the sign of The Blue Lantern, his old piano bar of many years earlier. He tried to fight off the temptation. He wanted to go in and check the old place out.

"No," he tried to tell himself, "don't do this."

The temptation was too strong.

He pushed the door a little bit. He took in the scene before fully opening the door and entering. It was the same, the same table, the same musty smell, even the same piano that had meant so much to him back then.

Then he saw Sam come out of the back room, a little grayer than he used to be, but still very much Sam.

Sam!"

"Jack, what are you doing up during the day?"

"No, Sam, it's me Paul. Remember me?"

Sam stopped what he was doing and looked at him out of the corner of his eye. Sam knew Jack's real name was Paul. Sam knew everything. He never fully understood what happened all those years ago. He certainly didn't understand why Paul had suddenly switched to 'Jack,' but he went along with it. Now, after all these years being Jack, why was he suddenly Paul again?

Sam decided to play it safe.

"Paul, yeah, I remember you. It's been a while. What've you been up to?"

"Working," Paul said. "I'm still with Janey, though. She's still the greatest."

"Janey...." Sam trailed off. "Hey, that's great."

"Hey, you...you think I could play the piano a little?"

"Sure, of course."

"I'm a little out of practice."

Paul sat down on the bench. He did a couple of runs up the keys to warm up. Then he began a slow melody

It was all there for him. He couldn't believe it. After all these years, he thought to himself, I feel like I haven't missed a day.

He played for about twenty minutes and asked Sam if he could come back later that night. Sam said of course, and Paul ran home to recap the crazy day for Janey.

She took the news in stride. She worried that Paul was pushing himself to the edge again, but she couldn't deny a twinge of excitement bubbling up deep within her.

At eight O'clock that evening Paul and Janey dressed for their evening out.

"Finally a chance to wear this skirt," Janey said. "I've been throwing it on the floor in my sleep for a couple of weeks now."

"Wow!" was all Paul could say. "you are beautiful. Come here."

They kissed.

The thought passed through Paul's mind that she really did look like the woman who called him Jack the previous morning. He pushed the thought away and looked at his beautiful wife. They were both a little worried and excited.

"Let's go," Paul said.

Sam had warned their friends at the bar not to call them Jack or Chrissy. They had talked about it before. Sam had told them about the old days, about the name changes. They didn't fully understand, but Jack was a good friend, and they all went along with Sam's advice.

Paul and Janey entered quietly and said hi to Sam. Sam gave Janey a friendly kiss on the cheek, and they sat down at a table near the far wall.

Randy and the others, at their usual table, glanced nervously in their direction. They talked in half whispers to each other.

After about ten minutes Paul finally gathered enough nerve to sit at the piano. He was a little stiff at first, notably less comfortable than he was earlier in the day. By the end of the first song, though, he managed to loosen up. From that point on, the music flowed through him.

Sam decided Janey shouldn't be sitting alone, and brought her over to the table with the others. He introduced her. She was shy but polite. Randy the others were confused, but acted as if they did not know her.

After a few songs Paul took a break and came over to sit with them.

"You play great," Suzy said.

"Thanks," he said.

She searched for any sign that he knew her. She saw none. She looked down in frustration.

"You ever met a guy named 'Jack'?" Randy asked boldly.

The others at the table gasped.

"No," Paul said, "but it's funny. You're the third person in the last couple days who's mentioned that name."

"Yeah, you're a lot like him," Randy said.

The mood lightened as the evening wore on. Eventually Paul went back to the piano. This time Janey followed and sat next to him. She began to exude a sensuality that caught Paul unprepared. He couldn't believe it; after feeling so flat and so non-sexual for so many months, here he was losing his mind over his wife.

He played with a sense of purpose. For the first time in many years he felt strangely at home with himself. It was all so natural, why had he denied himself this?

After another half-dozen songs he took another break. This time as he and Janey sat down with the others, the mood was relaxed and the group laughed easily at each other's stories.

Evening quickly gave way to midnight, and midnight gave way to the wee hours.

At four in the morning Paul and Janey were in the door for their bedroom kissing, groping, and undressing each other.

The night had been overwhelming for both of them.

Paul fell asleep just as dawn began to flicker to light outside. He hadn't felt so peaceful in years. He felt light. He felt alive. He drifted off into a happy sleep, which quickly turned into a deep deep slumber.

Just as his slumber reached its deepest point, he rose abruptly from the bed. He swung his feet to the floor and stood up. He grabbed the shirt with the cigarettes in the pocket, put on the closest pair of pants, shoved his feet into some shoes, and went outside.

Jack lit a cigarette and adjusted his eyes to the daylight. He couldn't remember the last time he had been out during the day.

He turned down the street and started walking.

After walking for several blocks, he stopped in front of a restaurant and looked at the sign. It said "The Salvador Deli." He stood for a good three minutes before shaking his head and moving on.

He continued down the street another four or five blocks. This time he stopped in front of Salvador's major competitor, "The Deli Llama."

Jack squinted, took a deep breath, and stood up straight, adjusting his shoulders slightly. He walked to the door, opened it, and approached the man behind the counter.

"Can I help you?" The man asked.

"Yeah," Jack said, glancing quickly around the deli's seating area. "I'd like to apply for a job."

www.ingramcontent.com/pod-product-compliance
Lightning Source LLC
Chambersburg PA
CBHW020619300426
44113CB00007B/704